Confrontation Talk

Arguments, Asymmetries, and Power on Talk Radio

Confrontation Talk

Arguments, Asymmetries, and Power on Talk Radio

Ian Hutchby
Brunel University, UK

Routledge
Taylor & Francis Group
NEW YORK AND LONDON

First Published by
Lawrence Erlbaum Associates, Inc., Publishers
10 Industrial Avenue
Mahwah, New Jersey 07430

Transferred to Digital Printing 2009 by Routledge
270 Madison Ave, New York NY 10016
2 Park Square, Milton Park, Abingdon, Oxon, OX14 4RN

Cover design by Mairav Salomon-Dekel

Library of Congress Cataloging-in-Publication Data

Hutchby, Ian
Confrontation talk : arguments, asymmetries, and power on talk radio / Ian Hutchby
p. cm.
Includes bibliographical references and index.
ISBN 0-8058-1796-4 (c). – ISBN 0-8058-1797-2 (p)
1. Talk shows–Great Britain. I. Title.
PN1991.8.T35H88 1996 95-50277
791.45'6–dc20 CIP

Publisher's Note

The publisher has gone to great lengths to ensure the quality of this reprint but points out that some imperfections in the original may be apparent.

Contents

Editors' Preface

The case studies included in the "Everyday Communication" series examine human communication behavior as a patterned process occurring within particular cultural and social contexts. *Confrontation Talk: Arguments, Asymmetries, and Power on Talk Radio* by Ian Hutchby is the third volume to appear. Actual conversations (in the form of transcript data) from talk radio shows take center stage in this book's analyses.

Hutchby uses conversation analysis to examine verbal confrontation as it occurs in a single context, talk radio shows that are broadcast in England. As talk radio reaches a larger audience, not only in England but in the United States and other parts of the world, research that treats its institutional and structural aspects seriously is welcome. This is particularly the case when we consider the potential influence talk radio has on and through other media (as in similarly conducted talk television shows on the one hand, and newspaper articles and television reports about discussions that occur on talk radio on the other).

Confrontation plays a central role in talk radio. By choosing to focus on confrontation, Hutchby not only illuminates our understanding of how arguments develop on talk radio, but he offers conclusions that apply to arguments in other contexts as well. Hutchby demonstrates that arguments are interactional accomplishments: They require the active participation of all the communicators. One cannot have an argument alone. Despite the fact that participants disagree on content, they must agree, in at least a limited way, about the formal constraints of the genre in order to have an argument.

Hutchby's study quickly turns into an investigation of power, particularly what happens when power appears unequally distributed among participants in an interaction. By definition, the caller and the radio host have unequal status, implying differential ability to initiate, sustain, and terminate arguments. Investigating this asymmetry, Hutchby shows how power works subtly, in everyday contexts, running through even brief conversations between strangers. This is not an overview of large (but largely unseen) social forces, but a careful study of how the words used between two individuals display and reinforce inequities.

Confrontation Talk thus brings the study of social forces to an accessible level: We may not all be callers to talk radio shows, but we have all participated in arguments in some context; close examination of talk reveals the mechanisms that some communicators may employ to initiate, exacerbate, moderate, and/or terminate confrontation. Everyone has experienced conversations that developed into arguments, wondered how exactly that escalation occurs, and how it sometimes can be prevented. Hutchby guides us through the process, showing how interruption is used as a strategic tool, and how this and other strategies can be resisted.

In short, using talk radio as his context, Hutchby provides a study of institutionalized power—how it is displayed and how it is reproduced in conversation. He does not offer broad generalizations about the nature of power; he shows us in specific, concrete detail.

Wendy Leeds-Hurwitz
Stuart J. Sigman

Acknowledgments

A great many people have given me the kind of help, encouragement, criticism, intellectual challenge, and support without which I would probably not have begun, let alone finished, this book. I would like to thank Colin Sparks at the University of Westminster, for whom I worked as a research assistant during the time when the original idea of studying arguments on talk radio shows occurred to me. The fact that he allowed and even encouraged me to develop this line of research, which was completely unrelated to the work I was doing for him, coupled with the fact that he undoubtedly had serious reservations about my methodological move toward conversation analysis (CA), both testify to his great intellectual generosity.

Also for continuing intellectual generosity, I would like to thank Paddy Scannell at the University of Westminster. During the same early period, his selfless donations of personal time, advice, and enthusiasm for Harvey Sacks' work were invaluable to me as I first fumbled with the literature of CA. Paddy was, and remains, important in encouraging me to continue with the work of applying CA to the language of the media.

During my doctoral research at the University of York, Paul Drew did his level best to train me in the hard grind of actually doing CA. His careful, considered, and always incisive comments and criticism of my work have been crucial not only in developing my own analytical skills, but also in shaping many of the analytic directions taken in these pages. His influence pervades the book, although I have no doubt that he would not agree with many of the things I use that influence to say.

At the University of Surrey, where the bulk of the work on the book was done, Nigel Gilbert was another generous boss who allowed me far more intellectual space and academic time than I first anticipated, in order to get the book finished.

A special mention must go to Robin Wooffitt, erstwhile colleague at Surrey and continuing friend, who was the one who talked me into writing this book in the first place. For his cajoling, as well as for one or two stylistic leg ups, I thank him.

The book is dedicated to Joanna Thornborrow, who has seen it through with me, and a lot else besides. Both personally and intellectually she has been, and remains, an inspiration.

Two of the chapters included here are extensively revised and updated versions of previous publications. My thanks to the British Sociological Association for permission to include, as chapter 4, a version of my paper "The Pursuit of Controversy: Routine Skepticism in Talk on Talk Radio" (1992), published in *Sociology, 26*(4), pp. 673–694. And my thanks to Sage Publications for permission to include, as chapter 5, a version of "Confrontation Talk: Aspects of 'Interruption' in Argument Sequences on Talk Radio" (1992), originally published in *Text, 12*(3), pp. 343–371.

All of the transcripts of the *Brian Hayes Programme* included herein are my own. All names of people and places have been changed.

Ian Hutchby

1 Talk Radio and the Discourse of Argument

This is a study of how arguments are conducted in a particular social setting: an open-line radio phone-in broadcast, or talk radio show. Open-line talk radio shows are notorious for generating a high degree of controversial and confrontational talk between their hosts and the callers—ordinary citizens, for the most part—they encounter. This notoriety extends deeply enough into Anglo-American culture for it to have provided the focal point of a movie released in the 1980s, *Talk Radio*. That film centered around the daily life and work of a controversial talk radio host whose character, although fictional, was loosely based on a real-life host, Alan Berg. Berg generated such controversy through his show that he ended up being shot by a vengeful listener.

Thus, when I decided to begin researching the interactional properties of argument, and was casting around for likely sources of data, an argumentative talk radio show seemed a good idea. In Britain (where the research was done) the most well-known talk radio show at that time was *The Brian Hayes Programme*, a daily show on London's LBC station. Hayes' propensity for skepticism and sarcasm was notorious enough that a profile for the national magazine *Radio Times* (Purves, 1991) described his show in these terms:

> For 14 years his reign of terror stretched across Greater London, as he daily pulverised Dave from Dalston and Janice from Walthamstow with terrifying put-downs and rebukes like, "A teeny bit muddled there" or, "You keep on saying that" or, ultimately, "We've gone through this several times, and if you don't understand now you never will." Click. (p. 18)

I randomly recorded nine entire broadcasts of the Brian Hayes phone-in, and ended up with a corpus of just over 120 calls.[1] These calls (not all of which involve Hayes as the host; in fact, three different hosts appear on the tapes I have) comprise the principal database for this book—although for comparative purposes I occasionally draw on other sources of data such as telephone conversations between friends, psychotherapeutic conversations, televised news interviews, and others.[2]

I considered talk radio to be a data source with distinct advantages over others used by researchers on argument, such as taped family discussions (Billig, 1991; Schiffrin, 1985; Vuchinich, 1990), recordings of children's play either on the street (M. H. Goodwin, 1990) or in the nursery (Corsaro & Rizzo, 1990; Eisenberg & Garvey, 1981), or recordings made in some kind of laboratory setting (Lein & Brenneis, 1978). The reason for this is simple: Although the participants were undoubtedly conscious of the fact that their talk was being broadcast to an overhearing audience, I took it that they could not reasonably be said to be aware—or to suspect—that some particular member of that audience was taping the proceedings in order to engage in sociological analysis of their talk. Essentially, what I captured on my tapes were interactional episodes that were as unaffected as they could possibly be by my presence as a researcher. That is, each of the broadcasts I recorded contained talk that would have been produced just the same if I had not turned on the tape recorder that morning. (Indeed, I recall listening to some broadcasts on mornings I had not elected to record, deeply regretting my decision, because they seemed to contain such good examples of argumentative talk!)

Yet the fact remains that the arguments I had recorded took place in a particular kind of setting: not in the family home or the psychology lab, but on the radio. Radio is of course a principal medium of mass communication, and media analysts in the past have shown some interest in studying talk radio as a mass communication phenomenon. The kinds of questions that have been asked, however—such as how effective is talk radio as a democratic forum, or how does it influence public opinion—are quite different from the questions that animate my research. I am interested in analyzing the actual *talk* that is at the heart of the talk radio show, without which, indeed, there could be no such thing as a talk radio show. As I have said, that talk involves argument as

[1]I should perhaps note that at the time of writing, the *Brian Hayes Programme* has been canceled by the broadcasting company. Although Hayes was remarkably popular, and his show had run for 14 years, one apocryphal story had it that his style was too abrasive and controversial for the radio company's attempt to construct a "new image" in the early 90s. Hayes subsequently went to work for BBC Radio 2, possibly the least abrasive radio station imaginable within the British broadcasting context.

[2]Throughout, I have tried to indicate in the text from what kind of setting cited examples are drawn, usually by stating that the extract is "from a conversation" or "from a news interview." In the case of the talk radio examples, it's made even more evident by the fact that the speakers are always designated "Host" and "Caller" in transcripts.

a central activity. But a second theme of this book considers how the arguments that take place can involve a particular set of power relationships between the two participants: the host and the caller. In the empirical chapters of the book one of the things I will do is to trace the social forces at work associated with these asymmetrical participant statuses, because these footings carry with them an unequal distribution of resources for initiating, sustaining, and terminating arguments.

The analytic approach I take comes from the perspective of conversation analysis (CA).[3] CA has two key methodological features. The first is its basic aim: "To describe the underlying social organization—conceived as an institutionalized substratum of rules, procedures and conventions—through which orderly and intelligible interaction is made possible" (C. Goodwin & Heritage, 1990, p. 283). The second is its central belief that that underlying social organization need not be reconstructed from field notes or members' reports on social happenings, as in traditional ethnography. Rather, it is directly available to observation in the details of naturally occurring interactions, which can be recorded using audio or video equipment (Sacks, 1984).

Accordingly, throughout the book, I base my analyses on recorded actual calls to a talk radio show. Transcripts of these calls are reproduced not just as illustrations, but as part of my analysis. They should be read as such, because I am dealing with events occurring in the real world, and the ultimate criterion by which my account may be judged necessarily lies in the organizational detail of those events. Of course, the transcripts themselves are only one kind of rendition of real-world events; but they allow the reader as far as possible, within current technological constraints, to match my interpretations to the details of the data on which they are based—and of course, if necessary, to disagree with me.

ANALYZING TALK ON TALK RADIO

This is not the first time that talk radio—or public-access broadcasting more generally—has been subjected to sociological and communicational analysis. Analysts in the past have brought a range of questions to bear on this genre of broadcasting. But this is the first time that talk radio has been studied from the distinctive perspective of conversation analysis. Consequently, many of the questions I will be asking about the data in this book are somewhat different from those that have previously been addressed.

A central focus in previous studies has been the question of how "demo-

[3]A general introduction to the perspective and method of conversation analysis is provided in Hutchby and Wooffitt (in press). Shorter introductions can be found in Levinson (1983) and in Heritage (1984).

cratic" talk radio is. These analyses tend to come from a media studies perspective, and focus on the fact that talk radio (and counterpart audience participation shows on TV) can be seen as a means of providing ordinary citizens with access to the public sphere represented in large part, in modern society, by broadcasting. Many years ago, the playwright and radical Bertolt Brecht (1932/1964) put forward the idea that "The radio would be the finest possible communication apparatus in public life, a vast network. . . . That is to say, it would be if it knew how to receive as well as to transmit, how to let the listener speak as well as hear, how to bring him into a relationship instead of isolating him" (p. 52).

To some extent, these possibilities are realized in the talk radio show. And this has led some media analysts to try and assess the extent to which talk radio in fact functions as a democratic forum. For instance, both Crittenden (1971) in one of the earliest studies, and Verwey (1990) in a more extensive, book-length treatment, explicitly address the democratic functions of talk radio, by examining the degree to which arguments put forward in talk radio discussions permeate the wider population of the overhearing audience, or by evaluating how different talk radio hosts facilitate open debate between themselves and members of the public.

But from the standpoint I adopt in this book, there is something radically missing from these studies of talk radio as a democratic forum (see also Avery & Ellis, 1979; Rancer, Miles, & Baukus, 1994; Step & Rubin, 1994; Turow, 1974). Nowhere in these studies does one find a consideration of the actual *talk* that talk radio shows broadcast. For instance, Verwey (1990) presents no examples of words actually spoken, or an exchange actually broadcast, during the many shows she recorded for her database. Verwey's preferred method is to transform the words people spoke into coded units or categories, such as expressions of opposition or support for some proposition, and then quantify the results in order to represent those positions in statistical tables.

This statistical approach does tell us something, albeit on a relatively gross level, about certain types of patterns in talk radio discourse, for instance, patterns of agreement and disagreement with various propositions, or at least patterns of positive and negative viewpoints given airtime by the show's producers. But, in the process, it leaves completely out of account the underlying question of the actual, situated speaking practices by which citizens' opinions on issues, and their debates with hosts, are managed in the public arena represented by the talk radio show. In other words, the talk that is at the heart of the talk radio show—through which, indeed, the talk radio show is constituted—is taken for granted as a window on underlying sociological variables, rather than being treated as a topic of analysis in its own right.[4]

[4]This observation relates to a long-standing issue in social science methodology about the relationship between language and reality, which has been discussed at length since the 1960s in a series of important texts, among them Sacks (1963), Garfinkel (1967), Garfinkel and Sacks

There have been other studies that have avoided this pitfall, and focused on the central role of talk in talk radio shows and their television counterparts. One of the earliest was by Moss and Higgins (1984). Their interest was in the ways in which different roles or discourse identities are embodied at different moments in the talk of hosts and callers to a talk radio show. To conduct this analysis, it was necessary to consider some actual examples of radio talk. Using Halliday's (1978) linguistic model of register, Moss and Higgins began to reveal the relationship between cultural knowledge and communicative intentions in actual talk radio discourse, and showed both the expressive dimensions of that discourse and the way in which the medium itself has a language whose features it is possible to delineate empirically. In short, Moss and Higgins' approach contributed to a shift in attention in media studies toward the question of *how* talk radio interaction is conducted, which is one of the central themes underlying the present book (see also Scannell, 1991).

This tendency is also evident in Carbaugh's (1988) study of the TV debate show *Donahue*. Here, the theme of democracy and the kind of public sphere being created by these shows again emerges, but in a different way from the survey-based statistical studies mentioned previously. Carbaugh suggests that one kind of significance of the public discourse of shows such as *Donahue* is that it can tell us a lot about the symbolic patterns and cultural structures of meaning circulating in mundane civil society: "Just as we have learned about Roman society by studying orations in the Assembly, and Colonial society by studying negotiations in the town hall, so we should learn much about contemporary American society by studying the kind of talk that is heard on *Donahue*" (p. 4).

Carbaugh takes an anthropological approach to the talk of debates on *Donahue*, using the contributions of audience members as a trace for the cultural categories and symbolic systems that circulate in contemporary American culture as a whole. He shows how, in the contributions of ordinary audience members, complex cognitive models of the self, authenticity, and "communicating" can be found. Thus, the discourse of *Donahue* interfaces the public and the private not only in terms of being the public talk of private citizens, but also in the sense that it illustrates the routine reflection of wider social patterns of reasoning in the speech of individual participants.[5]

Most recently, Livingstone and Lunt (1994), again focusing on TV debate shows, have been concerned with the contribution such shows make to the creation of a modern, mediated public sphere. In addition to analyzing the relationship between private and public themes and dimensions in the talk, Livingstone and Lunt discuss a number of dimensions such as the relationship

(1970), Zimmerman and Pollner (1971), Gilbert and Mulkay (1984), Pollner (1987), Moerman (1988), and M. H. Goodwin (1990).

[5]This theme has also preoccupied the social psychologist Billig (1991) in his work on everyday rhetoric and argumentation.

between expert and lay perspectives (and the way in which these shows subordinate the former to the latter), the relationship between abstract argument and lived personal experience in discussions of issues, and the broader political question of the media management of debates and consequences for the kind of participatory space that such shows in fact open up for the public.

The principal contribution these studies make, from my point of view, is to take seriously the fact that what talk radio broadcasts and their television equivalents consist of is, above all, talk. More specifically, they consist of what Goffman (1981) dubbed "fresh talk," talk that in general does not involve the speaker recalling memorized texts or reading aloud from a text, talk that is more or less spontaneous and, crucially, sensitive to its immediate context of production.

However, there are numerous ways in which the role of talk in such settings can be approached. In the studies just mentioned, the main concern is with how the content of the talk itself relates to wider social and cultural issues. Less attention is paid to the question of how that talk is actually produced, to the interactional and sequential contexts in which different participants speak, and to the relationship between the talk and the local organizational constraints of the setting itself. It is these latter three interests that represent my principal concerns in this book.

One of my main interests in the following chapters is in how sequential patterns in talk reveal participants' construction of social realities and communicative activities, and their orientations to social contexts and identity relationships. Beginning from this perspective, I will analyze the ways in which the communicative activity of arguing is practically accomplished through sequences of talk within the social setting of talk radio. In line with the general policy of conversation analysis, I will begin by bracketing the commonsense assumption that organizational features of talk radio, and/or the specific identity categories of host and caller, are *automatically* relevant for the course and outcomes of the interactions I recorded. This is not to deny that such factors may be relevant. In fact, one of the things I will show is that they are. Rather, it is to emphasize that the discovery of their relevance must be an empirical matter (Schegloff, 1991).

As this chapter proceeds, it will become clear that I aim to reveal the fundamental impact that organizational structure and the operation of power have on the trajectories of calls in my data. I will seek to show the way that the talk radio format itself is structured to promote a certain type of argument and confrontation. And I will examine how, as a consequence of this, the framework of interaction within calls functions to both enable and constrain the particular kinds of argumentative activity available to and undertaken by hosts and callers. This, I will argue, represents a way in which we can articulate the relationship between talk, asymmetry, and power in the discourse of social institutions.

In the rest of this introductory chapter, I outline in more detail just what all this entails. Beginning with a discussion of talk radio as a form of "institutional" discourse, I then discuss some broad themes in the conversation-analytic approach to that form of talk, before moving on to suggest how my analyses in this book will make a contribution to CA-oriented research by adopting its fundamentally local, sequential approach to address the question of power in institutional interaction.

TALK RADIO AS INSTITUTIONAL DISCOURSE

Talk radio is a form of institutional interaction. The talk takes place within an organization, the broadcasting company, which has its own structure and stability. That structure and stability are themselves phenomena which are produced and reproduced through talk and interaction (Boden, 1994; Drew & Heritage, 1992). The activities of the organization's members at all levels, from executive offices to the production floor of the studio, operate to provide the environment in which the host–caller interactions analyzed in this book can take place. Yet the talk and the interaction of calls themselves has an institutional character of its own: It is not just by virtue of being "talk in an institution" that talk radio is a form of institutional discourse.

How can we characterize the institutional nature of talk radio interaction? As Goffman (1961) once pointed out, institutions are things that sociologists "do not have a very apt way of classifying" (p. 15). But those who have studied talk in institutional settings in recent years have focused on two core features of that form of discourse: Institutional encounters are seen as "basically task-related and they involve at least one participant who represents a formal organization of some kind" (Drew & Heritage, 1992, p. 3).

Calls on talk radio possess both these features. The interaction is task-related in the sense that the talk is principally designed to discuss personal opinions about public issues. These discussions in turn take place in the context of telephone calls between ordinary citizens, who tend to be speaking from the private domain of their homes, and a host who both occupies the specialized space of the studio and is an employee and public representative of the broadcasting organization.

At the same time, however, the institutional space in which talk radio interactions take place is somewhat unique. It is a space created at the interface of private and public spheres of modern society. In calls to talk radio shows, a specialized form of talk—talk about personal opinions of public issues[6]—is

---

[6]This is not to say that such a form of talk is specialized in the sense of being *restricted* to this particular context. Clearly, people discuss their personal opinions of public issues in all sorts of places and for all sorts of reasons. But in the open-line talk radio show, this form of talk is pretty much the only type that gets produced. It is in this sense that I refer to it as specialized.

produced by two individuals respectively occupying what Scannell (1991) describes as the "completely separate . . . places from which broadcasting speaks and in which it is heard" (p. 3). For the most part, in broadcasting, the studio represents the primary location from which broadcast talk emerges; it is "the institutional discursive space of radio and television" (p. 3). Listening and viewing, on the other hand, "[take] place in the sphere of domesticity, within the spaces of the household and normatively in the small, family living room" (pp. 2–3). On talk radio, the voices of ordinary citizens are carried from that domestic sphere into the institutional space of the studio, and then projected back again, via the radio, to the domestic sphere of the audience.

It is not, then, that both participants occupy an institutional space (e.g., as in medical consultations that take place in the doctor's surgery), nor that the professional participant comes into the private space of the layperson (as would be the case when the doctor visits a patient in his or her home). Rather, the talk takes place at, and at the same time constructs, a mediated interface *between* these spheres. This makes talk radio a rather special form of institutional discourse, and it represents one of the reasons for it being subjected to analysis in the pages of this book.

But the uniqueness of the discursive space of talk radio is only one reason why I believe it is important to analyze the talk that goes on within calls in the kind of detail that I do in the following chapters. Analyzing talk radio discourse not only tells us something about the nature of institutional interaction and the role of talk in the construction and maintenance of institutional contexts (a point to which I return in more detail later). Because I focus my attention on *arguing* as the central speech activity within calls, there is also the opportunity to discover new things about the interactional structures and processes associated with conflict talk itself.

Argument is a form of interpersonal conflict made possible by a fundamental feature of human social life: the fact that people can entertain and be committed to entirely competing versions of reality. The importance of competing versions of reality has always been crucial for the social sciences; for instance, that issue is at the heart of many of the social phenomena studied by mainstream sociology, such as ideologies, revolutions, and the management of deviance. But the question of the practical strategies, procedures, devices, techniques, and formulas that people actually use in situated, real-time disputes over competing versions only emerged comparatively recently (Grimshaw, 1990). Nonetheless, by now substantial literatures exist on the practices of disputing among children, in legal contexts, and in a variety of other settings such as the family, the neighborhood, the workplace, and in the media (Brenneis, 1988).

My interest in conflict talk on talk radio concerns how participation in these disputes can be *asymmetrical.* In institutionalized settings for dispute, one topic of interest might be the relationship between verbal patterns and resources used in conflict talk and the asymmetric social identities associated with the setting (bearing in mind that this is to be treated as an empirical question, and not as an a priori assumption). In this book, I will argue that the asymmetries we identify can be conceptualized in terms of the power of certain participants to engage in communicative actions not available (or not available in the same way) to others. One of my central claims will be that a CA approach can reveal, in fine detail, the ways in which arguments on talk radio articulate with, and are shaped and constrained by, the organizational parameters of the social setting in which they occur.

This concern with the relationships between patterns of conflict talk and the institutional setting of talk radio disputes raises two broader theoretical issues. The first is the question of how we are to approach the relationship between the small scale details of talk-in-interaction and "wider" social contexts for action. The second issue is that of how institutionalized power may be related to, and instantiated in, the local practices of talk-in-interaction.

TALK, ACTION, AND CONTEXT

The first of these issues, the relationship between talk and context, brings into play a broader sociological debate about the relations between agency and structure. In the wake of what Giddens (1979) terms the "linguistic turn" in sociology—the emergence of research paradigms that ceased to treat language as merely epiphenomenal and came to consider it as central to the reproduction of social relations and social structure—a large body of research has aimed to trace out the connections between the micro level details of situated interaction and more macro level, structural phenomena such as power, ideology, bureaucracy, class, and gender. Crucial to much thinking on this topic is Giddens' (1981, 1984) idea of the "duality of structure." Rather than seeing agency (i.e., people's actions) and structure (i.e., the relatively stable patterns of form and continuity in social systems) as disparate elements which compete for analytic attention, Giddens proposes that the two are interdependent. Social structure is treated as both a resource for people's actions and an emergent outcome of those actions. In Giddens (1981) terms, it is "both the medium and outcome of the social practices it recursively organizes" (p. 171).

This idea is very close to the one I adopt in the following chapters. The difference, however, is that Giddens does not demonstrate in any close empirical detail *how* the duality of structure operates. The approach adopted within CA, on the other hand, although closely related to Giddens' theoretical stance (Boden, 1994), aims to demonstrate the recursivity of agency and structure by focusing on the sequential details of talk-in-interaction. CA treats talk as a vehicle for social action, as the means by which social organization is mutually constructed and sustained in interaction, and hence as the principal strategic site in which we can investigate agents' orientation to and evocation of social context, in the sense of the features of social context informing their activities. In the following paragraphs, I will unpack these assertions a little.

Within sociology, at least, what distinguishes CA[7] is that it seeks to treat talk in and of itself as a structurally organized form of social action. CA approaches recordings of naturally occurring talk with the twin aims of (a) describing the structural organizations informing its production, and (b) thereby explicating the methods used by interactants to engage in mutually intelligible courses of action. The complementary emphases on the internal structure or design of turns at talk (C. Goodwin, 1981) and the organization of *sequences* of turns (Sacks, Schegloff, & Jefferson, 1974) reveal elementary features of the maintenance of shared understanding or "intersubjectivity" (Schegloff, 1992), and the procedural means by which activities are coordinated within, and as part of, social situations.

This approach to the social action dimensions of talk-in-interaction leads to a dynamic view of context, which works on a number of levels. In the first place, CA emphasizes that, for their producers, utterances are not produced as isolated actions but as actions embedded in an ongoing context of interaction. More than that, utterances are always doubly contextualized in the sense that they are both context-shaped and context-renewing. Actions are context-shaped because they are produced and understood in light of the context set up by preceding actions and interpretations. They are context-renewing because each in turn forms part of the context in which next actions will be produced and understood, so that the interactional contextual framework is constantly being renewed (or altered) by each successive action.[8]

Although this idea of context centers on the sequential contexts of talk-in-interaction, the concern with how context is an active accomplishment also underpins research that investigates the issue of talk and social structure (Boden & Zimmerman, 1991). This is best represented by studies of institutional settings such as courts of law (Atkinson & Drew, 1979), classrooms (McHoul, 1978), medical consultations (Frankel, 1984, 1990; Heath, 1992), media contexts such as television (Heritage, 1985; Heritage & Greatbatch, 1991) and radio (Hutchby, 1995), and business organizations (Boden, 1994). Here, CA makes a decisive break from conventional approaches that adopt a "con-

---

[7]It is important to note that although CA is currently much more widely accepted and understood in areas such as linguistics (particularly discourse analysis) and communication studies than it is in sociology, it in fact has a distinctly sociological lineage. Notwithstanding Levinson's (1983) claim that CA represents a fundamental part of the linguistic enterprise of pragmatics (see also Hutchby & Drew, 1995), the core questions that animate CA on the theoretical level are best understood as addressed to a sociological, rather than a linguistic, audience (Lee, 1987).

[8]See Drew and Heritage (1992) for a more detailed account of these ideas.

tainer" model of institutional contexts (Coulter, 1982). In the container model, the view is that whatever goes on within some institutional setting is linked to the interactional constraints imposed by that setting's already existing organizational structure. CA rejects such an assumption, and instead asks: "How do the participants display for one another their sense of this setting as a specialized one?" In other words, the emphasis is placed not on how the setting somehow determines the activities, strategies and procedures adopted within it, but on how those activities, strategies and procedures make available (for participants and analyst alike) the participants' orientation to, and reproduction of, the institutional features of the setting.

Bound up with this is a comparative perspective in which the turn-taking system for conversation (described in detail in Sacks et al., 1974) is treated as a benchmark against which other forms of interaction may be recognized by means of their distinctiveness. Sometimes this "foundational" approach to ordinary conversation is conceptualized on an ontological level (Heritage, 1989; Sacks et al., 1974). Conversation is treated as the primordial medium of face-to-face interaction, as the primary source for socialization of infants into the norms of a culture, and as possessing the full array of potential practices. This is in opposition to institutional interaction, which is characterized by a systematic reduction and/or specialization of the repertoire of practices.[9] Regardless of whether or not we accept this ontological reading, the comparative perspective remains methodologically useful, because it succeeds in revealing the participants' active orientation to context through a focus on the distinctive details of interaction in different types of environment.

This position will inform my analyses of talk radio interaction in the empirical chapters of this book. But the argument as it has been presented may be rather abstract. Therefore, it will be useful to illustrate the way it works with the help of a concrete example. Following is a transcript of a complete, and relatively short, call to the *Brian Hayes Programme,* which can be used to make a number of basic points. For instance, the talk is specialized in various ways, and this can be understood in terms of the notion that participants orient to, and thereby constitute, the institutional nature of the interaction by designing their turns in specific ways. More significantly, there are typical patterns of actions that recur in my data and are exemplified in this call. These patterns will subsequently provide a basis for many of the analytic points

[9]Because all cultures involve not only conversation but also talk that is not "conversational" in the sense outlined by Sacks et al. (1974), this can be seen as more of an assumption than an empirically demonstrated fact. I recall this view being argued quite strongly by Malcolm Ashmore during a seminar I gave to graduate and faculty members at the University of Loughborough. My view is that although it may be an assumption, it seems a pretty strong one. In relation to the question of language and the development of cultural competence, Ochs (1988) provides a wide-ranging description of the different social settings and verbal practices by which infants gain linguistic and cultural competence in a Western Samoan community.

made in chapters 3, 4, and 5. (Transcription conventions are presented in Appendix A.)

(1) H:21.11.88:6:1-2[10]

Host: Kath calling from Clapham now good morning.
Caller: Good morning Brian. Erm: I (li-) I also agree
that thee .hh telethons a:re a form of
psychological blackmail no:w. (.) .hhh Be:cause
the majority of people I think do know that
charities exist, .hh we all have our own
charities that we contribute to:, (.) .h we do
not have open ended pockets where we can keep on
doing this. .hh And to sa:y because you have a
credit car::d, .hh you just salve your conscience
by paying- sending in your number:, .phh I'm
sorry but I: think that's making people, (.)
appear very erm (.) la:zy.=
Host: =Well it's certainly not blackmail,
Caller: °hh° .hh Well it depends on how you look at it
Brian,=I ha[ve got three appeals-]
Host: [We:ll, it is not black]ma:il. D-Doesn't
matter how you look at it it isn't blackmail.=
Caller: =I: have got three appeals letters here this week.
(0.4) All a:skin' fo:r dona:tions. (0.2) .hh Two:
from tho:se that I: always contribute to anywa:y,
Host: Yes?
Caller: .hh but I expect to get a lot mo:re.
Host: So?
Caller: .h Now the point is there is a limi[t to ( )
Host: [What's that
got to do- What's that got to do with telethons
though.
Caller: hh Because telethons yesterda:y (0.6) e::rm was
appealing to people, (.) to: send in fo:r various
things.
(.)
Host: [[Yes and you- an-] [y-]
Caller: [[.hh They cost a l]ot to [ad]minister Brian
to [st]art with.=
Host: [y-]
Host: =Well of course it does. I mean you can't do
anything on that sca:le, .h erm: un-unless there
is adminstratio[n.
Caller: [Nearly everyone that (.)
contributes to ae: charity, (0.9) is giving

[10]For data sources, see Appendix B.

42 probably as mu:ch as they can affo:[rd.
43 Host: [Well a::ll
44 you do:: then Ka:th is just say well to hell:
45 with them: they spend it a:ll on administration
46 so I'm not going to give any money to them. .hh
47 No if yer watching um- a telethon .h an:d you
48 don't particularly .h want to give money, .h
49 well then you simply don't give money. .hh It's
50 actually not a very difficult thing to: (.) work
51 out. .hh Thank you very mu:ch, and we go
52 to...((next caller))

The first thing to notice about this exchange is that it consists of little more than an argument, bracketed by a minimal opening and closing. These opening and closing sequences, along with a number of features of the talk between them, represent sites at which we can begin to observe the encounter's institutional character.

The host opens the call in line 1. His[11] first turn already has an institutional or specialized quality to it, in as much as it is constructed as an "announcement." In most types of telephone conversation, the called party's first turn is an answer to the "summons" represented by the telephone's ring (Schegloff, 1968). Hence we find typical response utterances such as a simple "Hello?" or, more commonly in European countries (Houtkoop-Steenstra, 1991), self-identifications in which the answerer recites his or her name. In institutional settings, the first turn again consists of a self-identification by the called party, but this time usually in organizational terms, for example, "Police Department," "Sociology," or "Simpson's Automart, how can I help you?" In my data, the host begins by identifying not himself but the *caller*, by naming her and situating her in relation to a geographical location: "Kath calling from Clapham" (line 1).

Of course, when I talk about the first turn here I mean the first turn of the actual broadcast exchange between host and caller. Throughout, it will be this broadcast exchange that I refer to as the "call." But from the caller's point of view, by the time he or she gets through to the host, the call in a more general sense has already been in progress for some time. In modern broadcasting contexts, the caller will have previously encountered other institutional agents on the way to getting on the air—principally, operatives whose job it is to screen calls. Although I have no data on these encounters between putative callers to the show and call-screening operators, the likeli-

---

[11]Throughout the book, I will refer to hosts using the male pronoun. This is because all the hosts who appear in my data are indeed male. Callers, on the other hand, will be referred to by gender-specific pronouns (although in line with standard practice, actual names and place names have been changed).

hood is that the more usual form of opening for institutional telephone calls—a self-identification in organizational terms—will be used in this setting.

It is interesting to note that in a corpus of calls from an early American talk radio show,[12] I found that the host himself answered the telephone using the conventional organizational self-identification format:

(2) BCII:Red

1	Host:	Thirteen minutes before ten o'clock here o:n
2→		W.N.B.C, ((click)) Good evenin:g, W.N.B.C:,
3		(0.3)
4	Caller:	A:h. (0.2) Is that Brad Crandall?=
5	Host:	=Yes sir good evening.

It may or may not be that callers to this show got straight through to the host after being placed on hold automatically. Nonetheless, this example serves to point up the way in which the host's first turn in my data, in which the caller's name and geographical location is announced, displays its design for reception principally by the overhearing audience.[13] By constructing his first utterance as an announcement, therefore, the host displays an orientation to the broadcast nature of his encounter with the caller.

Following the announcement, the host initiates a greeting exchange with the caller. Here, from primarily addressing the audience, the host has turned to address the caller with a standard "Good morning"; this invites the caller to respond in kind, "Good morning Brian," (line 2) and so to move into the speaker's role.

It is not so clear what might occur after the completion of this greetings sequence. Because it is a two-turn sequence (greeting + greeting) and thus complete after the second turn, either speaker could conceivably take the next opportunity to speak. What happens next in my data, however, is quite systematic. The caller, as in this call, embarks on a relatively extended turn in which an opinion on some issue is presented. Overwhelmingly, this is done without any further prompting from the host. For instance, in line 2 of the extract, the caller moves without a pause from returning the host's greeting to presenting her opinion on the subject of telethons.

This brings in the second point illustrated by this example. Throughout my data, the arguments that hosts and callers engage in are embedded within a relatively stable overall structure that characterizes each call and that can be described in terms of a series of phases.[14] Calls have easily recognizable open-

---

[12]Recorded in New York City in 1967. Emanuel Schegloff was kind enough to provide me with these tapes and some of his transcripts, although the transcriptions that appear in this book are my own.

[13]There is also a sense, I think, in which it invites the caller herself to recognize that she is next up on the air.

[14]The phased structure of institutionalized encounters has been described for medical con-

ing and closing phases; within those brackets, to use Goffman's (1971) term, each of the participants orients to the accomplishment of specific tasks at given moments. If announcements and greetings represent the first phase of the call, then I want to refer to the presentation of the caller's opinion, beginning in line 2, as the second phase. At the beginning of this phase, callers are oriented to their role of "opinion-producers." This situates the host in a corresponding role of "respondent and potential challenger" to the caller's opinion. This, as we will see in chapter 3, represents the interactional and organizational basis for some distinctive argumentative asymmetries to be found on talk radio.

The third phase of calls might be said to begin when the host embarks on responding to the point of view put by the caller. In extract (1), this occurs in line 14, when the host responds to the caller's view that "telethons a:re a form of psychological blackmail" by overtly disagreeing with it: "Well it's certainly not blackmail." What follows during this third phase, here as elsewhere throughout the data corpus, is a relatively free exchange of speaking turns in which the host and the caller discuss or, much more frequently, dispute the issue in question.

Almost invariably, these dispute sequences are terminated at the same time as the call itself is brought to a close. That is, hosts and callers typically do not first try to reach a resolution in their argument, before moving on to a separate closing sequence. Frequently, the last turn of the call is both a move in the argument and a termination of the call. In line 51, we find the host indicating the termination of the call simply by saying "Thank you very mu:ch." Notice, though, that the caller does not play any role in negotiating the call's termination. The host thanks the caller and moves on to the next call after taking a lengthy turn of his own and without offering the caller an opportunity to respond to his disagreement with her position. This again is quite systematic throughout my data. Calls are terminated unilaterally by hosts (in only one case does the caller "hang up" on the host), often immediately after they have produced a turn in which they have disagreed with, or in some other way evaluated, the caller's position. By terminating the call unilaterally, without any exchange of goodbyes or any other form of bilateral negotiation, hosts (and in that one case, the caller) are able to highlight and preserve the argumentative, even confrontational nature of interaction within calls.

Calls, then, have a basic overall structure that can be described as a four-

---

sultations by Byrne and Long (1976) and for emergency calls to the police by Whalen and Zimmerman (1987). However, not all of these kinds of encounter lend themselves to description in terms of relatively strict phases. Heritage and Sefi (1992) report that their collection of encounters between first-time mothers and Health Visitors working under the aegis of the British National Health System were "substantially diverse in terms of their overall trajectories, the type or ordering of the topics raised and in terms of the 'tone' or 'rapport' achieved between the parties" (p. 365).

phase activity pattern. The first phase is the opening. After that, the caller takes what tends to be a relatively long turn to present a strong opinion on an issue he or she has selected (second phase). When the host judges that this opinion is complete, or fully enough presented, he begins to respond to the caller's position (third phase). During this phase the participants exchange turns relatively freely in what frequently take the form of disputes about the issue in question. Finally, the call tends to be terminated unilaterally, on the host's initiative, and often on a disputatious note (fourth phase).

It is the third of these phases that will be the substantive focus of attention in this book. I will be analyzing the kinds of strategies, procedures, devices, and techniques for engaging in argument that are found in this stage of calls. More specifically, I will be looking at how asymmetries in the distribution of those argumentative strategies emerge, are used as resources by the participants, and hence have consequences for the trajectories of talk radio disputes. This, then, brings us to the second theoretical issue I mentioned earlier: the question of how power can be analyzed as a feature of discourse.

ASYMMETRY AND POWER

Studies of institutional discourse often begin with the tacit assumption that institutional settings involve structurally asymmetrical forms of interaction and relations of institutionalized power, in contrast to the ideally equal nature of participation in ordinary conversation. Recently it has been recognized that this dichotomy between the symmetry of conversation and the asymmetry of institutional discourse runs the risk of both oversimplifying the nature of asymmetry and overlooking the many ways in which participation in conversation itself may be asymmetric. As Linell and Luckmann (1991) point out, everyday conversations can involve various asymmetries that are consequential for their courses and outcomes. These include asymmetries between the initiator of an action and its respondent, between participants' respective states of knowledge, as well as asymmetries in conventional rights to certain kinds of knowledge invoked in conversation. For instance, Sacks (1992, Vol. 2, pp. 222–228) discusses how, in conversational storytelling sequences, the storyteller has different rights to "experiencing" and feeling "emotions" about the recounted events than the story recipient.

All that having been said, however, empirical analysis has repeatedly revealed fundamental ways in which institutional forms of discourse indeed exhibit systematic asymmetries that mark them out from ordinary conversation. To take an example, in medical encounters, which have been the subject of a vast amount of research documenting asymmetries in institutional interaction (Maynard, 1991), one way of tracing the power relationship between doctors and their patients is by counting the number of questions that are asked by each participant, looking at the *type* of questions asked by doctors and patients, and/or counting the number of times a doctor interrupts a patient and vice versa. Large-scale asymmetries emerge from such exercises from which it may be concluded that doctors exert control over the concerns expressed within the consultation, and patients defer to the authority of the doctor by refraining from battling for such control themselves.

In a good deal of research, these kinds of asymmetries are considered unproblematically related to the participants' institutional identities. In line with the container model of context outlined earlier, the claim is often straightforwardly made that institutions "are characterized by . . . hierarchical relations of power between the occupants of institutional positions"; consequently, agents may act so as to "exercise the power which is institutionally endowed upon them" (Thompson, 1984, p. 165). Conversation analysts seek a less theoretically prescribed understanding of asymmetry and power. As I have already remarked, this understanding is based on analyses of participants' displayed orientations to institutional features of context, as shown in specialized design features of talk. Asymmetry and power are seen as oriented to, and produced by actual talk, rather than being predetermined by a theoretically established context.

Although CA is not in favor of the view that power relations somehow preexist and determine the course of actual concrete encounters, I believe that by focusing on the local management of talk, this approach can provide compelling accounts of how power comes to operate as a feature of, and be used as a resource in, institutional interaction. Even though the issue is more often than not left entirely implicit, a good deal of CA can be seen as dealing with a possible analysis of power, where power is viewed in terms of differential distributions of discursive resources. These resources enable certain participants to achieve interactional effects that are not available (or are less available) to others in the setting.

For instance, in Atkinson and Drew's (1979) courtroom studies, although the issue is not made explicit, the fact that the attorney always has the right to ask questions while the witness is restricted to answering those questions gives particular powers to the attorney. One of these is what Drew (1992) later described as the "power of summary." The questioner "has 'first rights' to pull together evidence and 'draw conclusions'" (p. 507), in other words, to define the meaning and the terms of a particular set of answers, which is something that the witness cannot do. "The witness is left in a position of addressing and trying to deal with the attorney's selection of which items to pull together: she has no control over the connections which are made . . . nor over the inferences which may be drawn from such juxtapositioning" (p. 507).

Because of the formal structure of examination proceedings in court, there seems to be little that the witness can do about this beyond attempting to use her answers to rebut the implications of the attorney's questions. But in other kinds of settings, there may be ways in which the questioner's power can be more strongly resisted. For instance, in a consultation with a doctor, it may be possible for patients to try and put the professional in the "weaker" answerer's position. However, as a number of studies have shown, patients are often complicit in the construction and maintenance of a power situation in which the doctor not only determines the topics that will be talked about, but also defines the upshots and outcomes of their discussions.

For example, Frankel (1984, 1990) observes that although there is no institutionalized constraint against patients asking questions and initiating new topics, these activities are overwhelmingly undertaken by doctors and not by patients. He argues that this asymmetry arises out of a tacitly negotiated state of affairs in which there are two significant features. The first is that doctors routinely open up restricted participation options for patients by asking particular kinds of information-seeking questions, for instance, those that require strictly factual responses. The second is that patients themselves orient to and reproduce this asymmetrical distribution of participation rights, by choosing to offer new information to the doctor largely in the form of additional components tagged onto a response to the doctor's question. By this means, they preserve the doctor's role as questioner and their own role as answerer, even when they are seeking to introduce new information.

In a similar vein, Heath (1992) shows how patients orient to and reproduce an asymmetry in participation rights during the consultation by systematically withholding responses to doctors' announcements of diagnoses. Announcing a diagnosis amounts to an "informing," passed from the expert standpoint of the physician to the patient, about some aspect of the latter's physical condition. Again, although there is no institutionalized constraint against patients responding substantively to this informing, Heath shows that patients routinely react at this point either with silence or with a short, downward-intoned grunt or "yeh." Withholding a response occurs even in cases where "the doctor provides an opportunity for the patient to respond to the informing by not only delivering the diagnostic information within a distinct utterance or turn at talk, but also by leaving a gap following the medical assessment in which the patient has an extended possibility to reply" (p. 240). Heath proposes that through this practice, patients tacitly act to sustain asymmetries between themselves and doctors by ceding control over the course of the encounter to the physician.

Unlike many studies using methods other than CA (e.g., those in the broader domain of sociolinguistics [Fisher & Groce, 1990] or critical discourse analysis [Fairclough, 1989; Thornborrow, 1991]), these accounts focus on the existence of asymmetries without going on to make explicit claims about power in institutional discourse. But that is not to say that those kinds of claims cannot be made. By showing how participants display an orientation to institutional settings by engaging in certain activities and refraining from others, CA can also be used to illustrate how power, in the sense of differential resource distributions, can be linked to those orientations. What is implied by the studies just cited is that oriented-to activity patterns, such as differences in questioning and answering moves, may themselves be intrinsic to the play of power in institutional interactions. What I want to do in this book is to develop that argument in much more explicit terms. By focusing on the sequential organization of calls on talk radio, I will show how an asymmetrical distribution of argument resources emerges as a result of that sequential organization; and I will argue that it is in these sequential environments that the play of power, and its resistance, emerges as an observable accomplishment.

PLAN OF THE BOOK

The rest of the book is organized as follows. In chapter 2, I develop a model of arguments as interactional accomplishments. Focusing first on conversation and then on institutionalized disputes, I show how a basic Action–Opposition sequence is at the root of the different forms of argument found in these settings. Finally, the case of talk radio is considered in the light of the mundane/institutional distinction.

The outcomes of this discussion serve, in chapter 3, as the basis for an analysis of asymmetry and power in talk radio disputes. In this chapter and throughout the book, I not only analyze power as it is achieved using available verbal resources, but also show that there are ways that powerful strategies, usually deployed by the host, can be resisted, and the tables turned.[15]

Chapter 4 concentrates on the skeptical nature of hosts' talk in my data, and presents a detailed analysis of one particular device used in the accomplishment of skepticism, and the construction of argument and controversy. In chapter 5, I focus on how "confrontation" itself may be accomplished in talk using the strategy of interruption. I discuss the ways in which hosts use interruption strategically to exert control over the argument while exploiting the interactional constraints of the setting. I also, once again, identify ways in which callers resist hosts' attempts to use interruption to control the argument. Chapter 6 explores a central locus of power on talk radio: the closing of the call. Because the arguments between hosts and callers are terminated simultaneously with the termination of the call itself, this represents a significant locus in which the host has the greater ability to define what will stand as the public "outcome" of a dispute.

Finally, in chapter 7, I assess what all this means in terms of our understanding of talk radio as institutional discourse; I outline in more detail the model of arguments, interactional asymmetry, and institutional power that has emerged in the empirical chapters.

---

[15]This, of course, is a view of power and resistance that is broadly in line with the ideas of Foucault (1977). I return to this discussion in chapter 7.

2 Analyzing Argument

In this chapter, I embark on the task of analysis by developing a model of arguments as interactional accomplishments. This will be done by focusing first on the building of opposition in conversational disputes. I will suggest that arguments can be viewed as constructed by means of a basic Action–Opposition sequence, which can be chained by a given Opposition move being treated as the Action move of a next sequence. Noting that opposition in conversational disputes may be mitigated or highlighted using different turn formats, I will move on to look at how the specialized speech-exchange systems operative in many institutionalized contexts for disputes lead to those disputes being systematically mitigated in various ways. Only after this will I bring in the talk radio data, and show that in terms of the Action–Opposition sequence, talk radio is a relatively conversational dispute form which nonetheless takes place within a stable institutionalized discourse framework.

ARGUMENT: THE ROLE OF OPPOSITION

"Argument" is a term that has numerous uses in ordinary language. As O'Keefe (1977) notes, we can speak of "making" an argument (putting a case for some position) and of "having" an argument (arguing *with* someone). This distinction is echoed in Schiffrin's (1985) more technical categories of "rhetorical" and "oppositional" argument. By rhetorical arguments, Schiffrin means single turns in which "a speaker presents an intact monologue supporting a disputable position" (p. 37). Oppositional argument occurs when two or more speakers openly engage in disputing over a position across a series of turns.

There may, however, be danger in sustaining too sharp an analytic distinction between making and having an argument. For one thing, as Jacobs and Jackson (1981) point out, rhetorical arguments can of course become part of oppositional arguments as speakers' positions are contested and opposing positions are taken up and argued for. Moreover, even rhetorical arguments are produced in some interactional context, and are addressed in particularized ways to intended recipients. They may seek to construct for their audiences a restricted field of interpretation, by deploying what Witten (1992) describes as "centripetal devices": "structures of information that turn in on themselves, close meaning down, license or authorize a particular set of messages, discourage plural readings" (p. 20). But the function of these features of self-reinforcement is to *persuade a recipient* as to the argument's validity. Hence it is important to look not only at how arguments are made, but also at how their recipients respond to them. Indeed, one of the features of argument that will be stressed throughout this book is the way in which a second speaker's response to a first speaker's turn can actually be the key element in starting an argument by treating that first turn as "arguable" (Maynard, 1985).

The distinction between making and having an argument remains significant, however, when it comes to the different approaches that are pursued in analyzing argument. For instance, there is a tradition in the study of argumentation, or rhetoric, that dates back to classical Greece and was revitalized in Europe with the work of Toulmin (1958) and Perelman and Olbrechts-Tyteca (1971).[1] This approach, which focuses on the rhetorical construction of cases, has always been concerned principally with how arguments are designed to persuade (Emlyn-Jones, 1987). Indeed the definition put forward in van Eemeren, Grootendorst, and Kruiger's (1987) textbook on argumentation theory explicitly links arguments and the expression of opinions with persuasion: "Argumentation is a social, intellectual, verbal activity serving to justify or refute an opinion, consisting of a constellation of statements and directed towards obtaining the approbation of an audience" (p. 7).

But this classical approach treats argument as a function of reason, as essentially an intellectual activity. In contrast, the approach I take in this book sees argument as an *interactional process*. The classical approach focuses on the ways in which arguments are made by single speakers, and pays little or no attention to the interactive role of opposition in the local construction of naturally occurring disputes. One of the suggestions that will be made in this chapter is that once we shift the focus toward opposition as the key feature of arguments, we can begin to account for how apparently innocuous and es-

[1]For more recent developments in this tradition, see Kopperschmidt (1985) and van Eemeren, Grootendorst, and Kruiger (1987).

sentially nonargumentative actions such as mispronouncing a word can be responded to by others in a way that makes them the starting point for stretches of argumentative talk.

As I will show, focusing on the role of opposition provides us with a framework for understanding arguments that can be applied in many different settings. I will use this model to point out the key features distinguishing conversational from more institutional forms of dispute, before turning my attention toward arguments on talk radio and using the same model to bring out some of the distinctive features of that form of institutional argument.

ACTION–OPPOSITION SEQUENCES

Studies of arguments as dispute sequences have stressed the crucial role of adversative activities such as challenge, contradiction, negation, and other forms of opposition (Coulter, 1990; Eisenberg & Garvey, 1981; M. H. Goodwin, 1990; Maynard, 1985). Eisenberg and Garvey (1981) see disputes in terms of what they call "adversative episodes": "The interaction which grows out of an opposition to [an antecedent event such as] a request for action, an assertion, or an action. . . . An adversative episode is a sequence which begins with an opposition and ends with a resolution or dissipation of conflict" (p. 150).

Eisenberg and Garvey's stress on resolution as a way of terminating disputes has been challenged by other research on children in peer groups (M. H. Goodwin, 1990) and among family members (Vuchinich, 1990), which suggests that arguments are in fact more likely to end in stalemate or stand-offs that enable participants to save face and move on to other activities. But their model of adversative episodes is important, as Maynard (1985) points out, for its stress on the emergence of arguments out of oppositions to antecedent events—what Maynard calls "arguable actions."

In Maynard's (1985) account, any interactional move can in principle be opposed; it can be treated as an arguable action and hence as the basis for starting an argument. The analytic focus is thus trained on the *oppositional* move as the key one in starting an argument. The first move in an argument sequence is also the second move in an underlying Action–Opposition sequence. Extending this slightly, we can think of arguments proceeding by means of opposition moves themselves being treated as arguable actions in further Action–Opposition sequences. This is not to say that arguments take the form of chained "paired-action sequences" in the same way in which many kinds of interview, for instance, are constructed out of chains of question–answer adjacency pairs[2] (Frankel, 1990; Greatbatch, 1988; for a paper that

[2]The concept of "adjacency pair" was developed in Sacks' (1992) lectures on conversation. A detailed description and application of the concept can be found in Schegloff and Sacks (1973).

defends such a view, see Coulter, 1990). The difference is that questions are actions that make specific action-types (i.e., answers) accountably relevant in the next slot. If an answer is not forthcoming, there should be some means of accounting for its absence. Oppositional moves, on the other hand, depend on the recipient electing to treat the prior turn as arguable: The absence of an oppositional move cannot be treated as accountable in the same way as the second part of an adjacency pair. In short, a question *projects* an answer slot, whereas an opposition *subsequently* formulates the prior action as an arguable.

Approaching arguments as Action–Opposition sequences in this sense allows us to investigate participants' use of locally emergent features of the talk in constructing their disputes. Among other things, we can look at the kind of actions that get treated as arguables and the sorts of normative cultural code that speakers utilize in identifying arguable actions (Maynard, 1985, 1986). We might also investigate the interpretive resources used by speakers in formulating and reformulating another's words and actions in the activity of "building opposition" (M. H. Goodwin, 1990).

This way of looking at things is not meant to deny that persons can "go looking" for an argument, for instance by trying to needle a coparticipant, making blatantly controversial claims, and so on. Nor is it meant to suggest that only recipients are ever active parties in treating a turn as arguable. Particularly once an argument is in course (but not only then), speakers may well make strong assertions with which they can expect others to disagree. Something of this kind seems to be what Coulter (1990) has in mind when he places "declarative assertions" at the heart of his model of argument sequences. Declarative assertions are described as "assertions designed to make some *point* to be addressed by . . . interlocutors" (p. 185).[3] It is important to note, however, that even though a speaker may produce a declarative assertion (or even go to the extremes of acting in an obviously perverse or contentious manner) the emergence of an actual argument is still dependent on the appropriate, oppositional response to these actions. And a recipient may elect (perhaps equally perversely) to ignore or even agree with the controversial assertion, thereby effectively neutralizing it.

In a similar sense, treating arguments as response-centered emergent events allows us to account for the fact that even apparently innocuous statements or actions can be treated as arguables and vehemently opposed. In his studies of children arguing during collaborative classroom work, Maynard (1985, 1986) illustrates how actions as apparently innocent (for their producers) as

---

[3]Coulter indeed argues quite explicitly that declarative assertions are first parts in an adjacency pair sequence (the "assertoric sequence"), with actions such as "agreement," "disagreement," or "counter-assertion" being relevant second parts (p. 186). As I have already suggested, I think this position is untenable because it mistakenly conflates the stronger prospective constraints operating for adjacency pair sequences with the weaker retrospective basis for the construction of what I prefer to call Action–Opposition sequences.

moving a pencil or mispronouncing the word "eraser" can form the starting point for extended stretches of disputation.

The basic point, however, is that approaching argument through the Action–Opposition model places the analytic focus squarely on the sequential organization of talk-in-interaction as the framework within which participants manage conflict talk. In the following sections of this chapter, I will use that model to discuss how the sequential management of disputes varies between informal conversational contexts and more formal, institutional settings. Beginning with some observations on the relationship between conversational turn-taking and the procedures by which the character of oppositional moves may be highlighted or downplayed, I will examine how institutionalized constraints on turn-taking and other aspects of participation come into play to modify the organization of disputes in settings such as courtrooms and news interviews. Following that, in the last part of the chapter, I will draw out some of the relevant features of argument sequences on talk radio, as a lead-in to the more specialized empirical chapters to follow.

ARGUMENTS IN CONVERSATION: AGGRAVATED AND MITIGATED OPPOSITION

In the following extract taken from an informal setting, two speakers, Al and Stan, are engaged in an argument about marijuana use. This fragment illustrates the operation of the Action–Opposition sequence in building a dispute. Al's assertion that "Marijuana is very cheap" (line 1) is treated as an arguable action by Stan, and he opposes it in the next turn by challenging Al's understanding of what "very cheap" might mean.

(1) Adato:7:17-18

1	Al:	Marijuana is very cheap.
2	Stan:	Very cheap at fifty cents a joint? an' a dollar
3		a joint? is very cheap?
4	Al:	You- about a- about a third of a joint gets you
5		high.
6	Stan:	So?
7		(1.0)
8	Stan:	The difference is that you need'm so much . . .

Stan initially opposes Al's position by challenging his competence in understanding the concept of "cheapness." By quoting prices for joints (line 2), Stan proposes that marijuana, far from being cheap, is in fact very expensive. Al counters this challenge by opposing it with the claim that one does not need a whole joint to get high. Thus, Stan's initial opposition (which treated Al's statement as an arguable action) becomes treated as an arguable action in a next Action–Opposition sequence. With this oppositional move, Al, like Stan before him, both undermines his opponent's position, in turn attributing incompetence in understanding how marijuana may be used, and at the same time provides a defense for the stance taken in his own previous turn.

However, the use of Action–Opposition sequences is not all there is to describing this fragment of talk as an argument. The specifically argumentative character of the talk can also be traced in the ways that oppositional moves are constructed in order to highlight, rather than downplay, their oppositional character. In M. H. Goodwin's (1983) felicitous term, Stan and Al engage in the exchange of "aggravated" opposition turns. Goodwin points out that opposition can vary in its intensity: Speakers can disagree with one another in a friendly or "mitigated" way, or they can disagree in more confrontational ways. It is the latter half of this scale to which Goodwin (1983) refers with the term aggravated opposition.

The aggravated nature of opposition can best be discerned by looking at a principal alternative means by which conversationalists engage in disagreement and dispute, by using techniques designed to mitigate and systematically deemphasize the oppositional properties of turns. Conversation analysts such as Pomerantz (1984a) and Sacks (1987) have contrasted the construction of turns designed to agree with the action in a prior speaker's turn and those designed to disagree with it. These design differences are described in terms of a preference organization: The format for agreements is labeled the "preferred" action turn shape and the disagreement format is called the "dispreferred" action turn shape (Pomerantz, 1984a, p. 64).

The concept of preference as it is used in CA is not intended to refer to the psychological motives of individuals, but rather to structural features of the design of turns associated with particular activities, by which participants can draw conventionalized inferences about the kinds of action a turn is performing. In Sacks' original use of the concept, in his lectures on conversation (Sacks, 1992), the preferred action was thought of as the default interpretation. One thing Sacks observed was how initial actions could be designed to "invite" a particular kind of response. For instance, the phrase "isn't it?" might be appended to an assessment, thereby inviting the recipient's agreement. In such cases, as in extracts (2) and (3), the default response gets produced straightforwardly and contiguously:

(2) JS:II:28

1	Jo:	T's- it's a beautiful day out isn't it?
2	Lee:	Yeh it's just gorgeous.

(3) VIYMC:1:2

1	Pat:	It's a really clear lake isn't it?
2	Les:	It's wonderful.

In contrast, turns that in some way depart from the default interpretation will incorporate any of a variety of "dispreference markers" (Pomerantz, 1984a). One of the most significant ways speakers have of indicating the dispreferred status of a turn is by starting the turn off with markers such as "Well," or "Um":

(4) Sacks, 1987

1	A:	You coming down early?
2	B:	Well, I got a lot of things to do before getting
3		cleared up tomorrow. I w- probably won't be too
4		early.

As Sacks (1987) observes, A's first turn here appears to indicate that he expects B to be "coming down early" (note the opposite expectation that would be conveyed by "You're not coming down early are you?"). The construction of B's noncongruent response exhibits two principal features of dispreferred disagreements.[4] First, the response is "formed up so that the disagreement is as weak as possible" (Sacks, 1987, p. 58). Notice in particular line 3, where "I w-," which looks like a start on "I won't be too early," is repaired to take the weaker form "probably won't be too early." Secondly, that actual disagreement is not produced early in the turn, like the agreements in extracts (2) and (3), but is held off until B has not only produced a "Well," but also has presented an account for *why* he won't be early (lines 2–3).

The upshot of this is that speakers may display an orientation to the potentially oppositional properties of disagreement, and possibly avoid opposition altogether, by utilizing the preference caveats to systematically deemphasize opposition. That does not mean, however, that disputes cannot be carried on while speakers are observing the preference caveats. They can, as the next ex-

[4]It is important to note that not all "dispreferred" turns involve disagreement. As Pomerantz (1978) discusses, after a turn that performs self-deprecation, disagreement is the default response and should be produced in a preferred turn format. For instance:

[Invented exchange]

A: I'm really no good at painting.
B: No, you're excellent, really!

If, on the other hand, you want to *agree* with another's self-deprecation, unless you want to appear harsh or rude, you should use a dispreferred turn format to do that agreement. Compare the following two exchanges:

(1) Invented exchange

A: I'm really no good at painting.
B: I know, you're atrocious.

(2) Invented exchange

A: I'm really no good at painting.
(Pause)
B: Well, I don't know. Maybe you could use some tuition. . .

tract shows. In this excerpt, a dispute goes on over a series of turns yet dispreference markers are used throughout to deemphasize opposition.

Gene is disagreeing with Maggie over her evaluation of the state of his marriage (lines 1–3). But note the differences with the argument sequence presented in extract (1). In each exchange, the disagreements are mitigated in various ways. For instance, Gene's disagreement with Maggie is delayed both sequentially, by a 0.8-second gap (line 4), and within the construction of the turn itself, by being placed after an "agreement preface" (Pomerantz, 1984a) (line 5). Similar features are found in the next exchange (line 8, line 9), and again toward the end of the extract (line 21, line 22):

(5) Goldberg:II:2:18

Maggie: A::n' uh::, .hh definitely, fo:r the: fifteen years
I:'ve known you, (0.3) you know you've really bo:th
basically honestly gone your own ways.
(0.8)
Gene: Essentially:: except we've had a good relationship
at [home you know.]
Maggie: [.h .hhhhhhhh]
(.)
Maggie: Ye:s but I mean it's a relationship where: uh
you know pa:ss the butter dear, hh
(0.5)
Maggie: You kno[w make a piece o' toa]:st dear this type=
Gene: [No not really.]
Maggie: =of thing.
(.)
Maggie: [[.hhhhhhhhhhhhhhhhh]
Gene: [[We've actually had a] real health- I think we've
had a very healthy relationship y'know.=
Maggie: =.k.hhh Why: because you haven't knocked each
other's tee:th ou:t?
(0.7)
Gene: Tha:t, a:nd we've::: had a good communica:tion
and uh: the whole- you know I think it's been
healthy,...

In this extract, although it is evident that the speakers are disagreeing with each other, it is also evident that neither is concerned to foreground that disagreement by engaging in aggravated opposition. In extract (1), however, Stan and Al's disagreements are not delayed sequentially by means of hesitation, nor are they pushed back in the construction of turns through the use of such things as agreement prefaces. Rather, each turn is concerned simply with doing the work of disagreement or opposition.[5] The very absence of

[5]There may be a sense in which it is possible to sustain an analytic distinction between the

markers of reluctancy or mitigation represents a means by which Al and Stan foreground their opposition and upgrade or intensify their conflict.

To summarize, then, the model introduced in this section represents the most useful way of conceptualizing and analyzing arguments as interactional accomplishments. The Action–Opposition model will underpin my analyses of talk radio disputes in subsequent chapters. So far I have focused on the function of preference caveats in the accomplishment of mitigated and aggravated argument forms. In order to see how all this applies to the case of talk radio, it is necessary first to situate my account in terms of the different constraints that affect the role of opposition in institutionalized disputes more generally.

INSTITUTIONAL DISPUTES: COMPARATIVE DIMENSIONS

As I noted in chapter 1, CA uses a comparative method to discover the specialized nature of institutional discourse. By means of this approach, CA has distinguished two basic types of institutional discourse: formal and nonformal (Heritage & Greatbatch, 1991). The formal types are represented by courts of law, many kinds of interview—particularly the broadcast news interview—certain kinds of classroom environment, and various ceremonial occasions. The point is to show that there is a close relationship between the social identities adopted by participants in these settings, and the forms of talk in which they engage. As Heritage and Greatbatch put it: "The institutional character of the interaction is embodied first and foremost in its *form*—most notably in turn-taking systems which depart substantially from the way in which turn-taking is managed in conversation" (p. 95). Typically, that turn-taking format involves chains of question–answer sequences in which the institutional figure asks the questions and the witness/pupil/interviewee provides the answers.

In the second type of setting, the nonformal type, much less uniformity in the patterning of conduct is evident. Studies of such environments as doctors' surgeries (Heath, 1992), psychiatric interviews (Bergmann, 1992), and various other social welfare encounters (Heritage & Sefi, 1992; Perakyla & Sil-

activities of "disagreement" and "opposition," where the latter is an activity fitted to argumentative contexts. Kotthoff (1993) goes some way toward making that distinction, by suggesting that the preference structures operative in "ordinary friendly conversation" (i.e., those described in Pomerantz, 1984a) are transformed once a "dissent turn sequence" begins. In this situation, disagreeing turns become the default case and get produced in preferred-action format, whereas turns that concede the other's point take a dispreferred-action format. The danger with Kotthoff's approach, however, is that of placing too much emphasis on the supposed objectivity of preference structures. As the previous few paragraphs have suggested, I think that it may be more useful to sustain a distinction between aggravated and mitigated opposition forms than between disagreement and argument as activity types.

verman, 1991) show that the turn-taking frameworks allow for much more variation, improvization, and negotiation for both institutional representatives and citizens/clients. In Drew and Heritage's (1992) term, the interaction has a "quasi-conversational" character. Thus:

> It is unlikely that a single recursive procedure (such as is found in special turn-taking procedures) can be found that would pinpoint the participants' turn-by-turn instantiation of institutional role-based identities at a single stroke. Accordingly, the participants' orientation to the institutional task- or role-based character of their talk will be located in a complex of non-recursive interactional practices that may vary in their form and frequency. (p. 28)

Within this framework, studies focusing on disputatious talk have mostly been concerned with settings at the formal end of the continuum, principally, disputes in legal settings (Atkinson & Drew, 1979; Drew, 1990, 1992) and in broadcast news interviews (Clayman, 1988, 1992; Greatbatch, 1988, 1992). In these studies, the principal distinctive features of the talk center around the ways in which the participants' institutional identities are linked with relatively formal constraints in the speech exchange system.

In Atkinson and Drew's (1979) study of trial courts, they coined the notion of "turn-type pre-allocation" to characterize the organization of interaction in trial courts. Subsequently, this was extended to the analysis of news interview turn-taking by Greatbatch (1988). Turn-type pre-allocation means that participants, on entering a setting, are normatively constrained in the types of turns they may take according to the particular institutional identities in which they are incumbent for the purpose of the encounter. Broadly speaking, both in courtroom examination and in news interviews, one party—the attorney or the interviewer—is restricted to asking questions, whereas the other principal participant—the witness or interviewee—is restricted to answering those questions.

But the turn-type pre-allocation format is only a minimal characterization of the speech exchange system for these types of institutional interaction. As Atkinson and Drew (1979) point out, any of a range of actions may be done in a given turn. The point, however, is that whatever those actions are, they are required to be done in the *format* of a question or an answer. At the same time, a further normative constraint operates to restrict the distribution of rights to express a personal opinion on matters under debate. That is, in neither setting are questioners accorded rights to take up a stance on their own behalf. Rather, their task is to elicit the stance, opinion, or account of the one being questioned, but to do so at least technically without bias or prejudice. This is because both courtroom and broadcast news talk are designed to be attended to principally by overhearing audiences: the jury (and in a slightly different sense, the judge) in a trial court, and the public in broadcast news. For different reasons, the audience in each case is supposed to draw inferences and make judgments about the one being questioned (or at least to be allowed to do so) without undue influence from the actions and opinions of the questioner. In fact, then, as well as constraints on the form of questioners' turns, there are also restrictions on their content, in as much as a turn should not be hearable as putting forward a personal opinion on the matter under discussion.

These constraints have a range of consequences for the organization of conflict talk as it occurs in these settings. First of all, the fact that actions such as challenging, accusing, or doubting have to be achieved within a question format means that questioners employ various strategies to do on an indirect or implicit level what speakers in conversation may elect to do straightforwardly. For example, in broadcast news, interviewers can produce talk that is critical and challenging toward interviewees by strategies such as embedding critical or evaluative statements within questions, citing the "facts" so as to emphasize their contrastive relationship with an interviewee's statement, or attributing opposing points of view to others and offering them for comment (Pomerantz, 1988–1989). These strategies enable interviewers to take up what amount to critical stances on their own behalf, while formally adhering to the journalist's norm of neutrality (Clayman, 1988, 1992).

Atkinson and Drew (1979) discuss another type of embedding strategy. In trial courts, a central task of attorneys, as representatives of one side in the case on trial, is to discredit their opponent's position and build support for that of their client. The only information attorneys have to work with in this pursuit is the testimony of witnesses, which in turn is produced in the form of responses to questions posed during examination and cross-examination. A central way in which attorneys imply a challenge, accusation, or blame-ascription is by managing the way in which events are described so as to "formulate the upshot of those descriptions in such a way as to propose a judgement about the witness' actions" (Atkinson & Drew, 1979, p. 134). In fact, formulating upshots of descriptions in this potentially critical way is a questioner's strategy that is also routinely used by news interviewers, as Heritage (1985) shows, and by talk radio hosts, as I show in chapter 3.

The communicative processes of implication and inference are thus routinely heightened in salience for conflict talk in courtroom and news interview interaction. This can be seen still more clearly if we turn to the activities of answerers in these sequences. Witnesses and interviewees will of course be sensitive to the impugnary undertones of many of the questions put to them, and will deploy strategies of their own to construct their answers as denials, rebuttals, accounts, and so on.

On this issue, Atkinson and Drew (1979) offer a detailed analysis of how witnesses undergoing cross-examination regularly produce defense-type components—justifications, excuses, or rebuttals—*before* the production by an attorney of an accusation or other impugnary action. Witnesses in short can display their orientation to a hidden agenda in attorneys' questions, that agenda representing an implicit position operating as the indirect but detectable motivation lying behind questioning strategies.

Some further ways in which speech exchange systems operating for particular settings impact on the management of disputes are detailed in Garcia's (1991) analysis of mediation hearings in a small claims court, and in Greatbatch's (1992) study of the panel set-up in some broadcast news programs, where a number of participants with varying stances on an issue act jointly as interviewees with the interviewer as chair.

In both these environments, disagreement is an intrinsic feature of the encounter. In Garcia's data, the official task of the mediator is to hear and arbitrate between two sides in an ongoing dispute which arose in circumstances external to the hearing, and which is now being brought into this setting for an independent decision to be passed. In a similar sense, Greatbatch (1992) notes that in panel interviews, interviewees are selected precisely on the basis of their differing standpoints on issues. Panel formats thus "allow interviewers to facilitate combative interaction through the airing of disagreements between the interviewees themselves" (p. 272).

However, the fact that in both cases there is a specialized distribution of speaker roles and rights leads to the disputes taking distinctive forms. In both settings an institutional agent (the arbitrator in Garcia's data, the interviewer in Greatbatch's) is accorded a central mediating role, with two main consequences. First, in both mediation hearings and panel interviews, the institutional agent is allotted the task of eliciting, through questions, the position or version of events supported by each antagonist. Consequently, oppositional turns are generally *not* adjacently positioned, because each side's opportunity to put forward its case needs to follow an intervening question from the mediator.

This has the important consequence that opposing sides in a dispute tend not to address their disagreements directly to each other, but instead to direct their talk at the mediator as a third party. As Garcia (1991) points out, in mediation hearings this feature takes the form of a sanctionable norm, in that disputants who shift into direct person-to-person opposition will be required by the arbitrator to readopt the footing of addressing the arbitrator and referring to codisputants in the third person. In the case of panel interviews, the convention is less stringently observed. Interviewers may allow interviewees to argue with each other directly for short periods of time. But as Greatbatch (1992) shows, there are various ways in which the interviewer retains overall control of the course of the dispute, and at any point he or she may reestablish the mediated format.

In all of these studies of institutional dispute procedures, the differences with conversational arguments are marked. First of all, the specialized turn-taking systems found in formal institutional discourse mean that the Action–

Opposition model, in which any action may be treated as an arguable and be opposed, appears only to fit in a modified way. For the most part, the question–answer sequence represents the most important framework for contributions, and this tends to overdetermine the formulation of arguable actions and oppositional moves. Secondly, the fact that opposition is constrained within these specialized turn-taking systems means that actual person-to-person opposition is systematically mitigated. I noted earlier that a feature of conversational argument is that participants may use preference caveats to mitigate opposition. In formal institutional settings, the fact that certain participants, usually the institutional representatives, have to refrain from expressing a personal opinion means that a significant form of mitigation is built into the dispute sequence itself.

Having made these remarks about formal institutional settings, I can now turn in more detail to the talk radio data. The earlier discussion provides a framework in which we can understand talk radio as a nonformal type of institutional setting for disputes, and thereby see how it is different both from conversation and from the formal settings. In fact, like most nonformal types (see Drew & Heritage, 1992), talk radio represents an "intermediate" category that manifests many of the sequential features of conversational argument in parallel with some relatively specialized institutional features.

ASPECTS OF CONFLICT TALK ON TALK RADIO

Aggravated and Mitigated Formats

As in conversation, oppositional turns on talk radio may freely take aggravated or mitigated forms. When opposition is mitigated, it is not through any constraints on turn-order or turn-type, but by means of the standard conversational strategies described earlier in this chapter.

For instance, in the following two extracts, hosts use the mitigating preference feature of agreement-prefaced disagreement (Pomerantz, 1984a; see line 4 in extract [6] and line 8 in extract [7]):

(6) H:30.11.88:3:1 ((The caller here is referring to senility among older members of the judiciary.))

Caller: I- I think, .h a ma:n of that a:ge, .h it's
obvious 'is brain doesn't function as well, .hh
as a man say hal:f 'is age.
Host: We::ll, yes but I'm frequently tol::d an:d I
frequently notice, that er some of these, .hh
y'know so call:ed e:rm slo:w thinking or, .h
brain defective people, .ph erm:, actually have
a great deal of wisdom and er, sharp lod- logic

and knowledge. . . ((so it isn't necessarily right to
accuse them of senility))

(7) H:30.11.88:5:2 ((The caller is complaining about a TV program about the death of a suspect in police custody.))

Caller: And e:r th- (.) they didn't address the actual
.p so much the actual events o:r what led up to
'em or how many- people wen' in:to the shop with
'im whether the man was intimida:ted whether 'e
tried to es:cape, .hhh and i- it was just an
a:nti police- (.) it was a police bashin'
exercise [(far as I-)
Host: [Well maybe- maybe it wa::s but I mean
from what you:'ve told me I: must admit I would
be a bit erm, .hhh to say the least shocked by::,
somebody being killed under those circumstances.

In contrast, in the next two excerpts, modulating features are almost entirely absent from the turns of both hosts and callers. In extract (8), among the ways in which opposition is foregrounded are the repeated use of turn-initial polarity terms, for instance "No [there isn't]" (line 10); and the use of straightforward inversion, as in the host's riposte to the caller's initial assertion that "there's no one voice for the blacks in [South] Africa": i.e., "There's no one voice for the whites either" (line 4).

(8) H:23.1.89:10:3

Caller: Look. (0.8) You know yoursel:f that there's no one
pa- there's no one voice for the blacks in Africa
is the:re. (.) .ph[h
Host: [U-er there's no [one voice for]
Caller: [i- if the]=
Host: =[the white- [There's no one voi]ce for the whites=
Caller: [A: N C, [I beg your par]
Host: =either.=
Caller: =W-there is at the moment, [there's the gover]nment=
Host: [No there isn't,]
Caller: =of South [Africa.
Host: [No there isn't.
(0.6)
Caller: Oh there's no government in South A[frica,
Host: [No, there is
not one voice I'm telling you, .hh that there are
a lot of partie[s,
Caller: [There's opinions in that voi:ce
different opinions in the voice but there is one
authority there.

In the next extract, the host and caller are disputing over what happened to the money generated by ticket sales for a reception honoring the Princess of Wales on a recent U.S. visit. Here, the opposition is foregrounded in a sequence in which, beginning with the caller's "But you don't know do you" (line 10), the antagonists confront each other with reciprocal accusations about each other's lack of knowledge on the issue (lines 16, 19, and 21).

(9) H:2.2.89:3:2

1	Host:	Well what d'you think it's going to.
2	Caller:	I've no- 'aven't a clu:e.
3		(.)
4	Host:	E:r, well if you haven't a clu::e,
5		you m[ight-
6	Caller:	[Ye:h well I mean whe:re d'you [think it's]
7	Host:	[you- you]=
8	Caller:	=[going] to.]
9	Host:	[might've]] I think it's going to charity.
10	Caller:	Yeh but you don't know do you.
11	Host:	Ehrm I'm almost su:re.
12		(.)
13	Caller:	We:ll,
14		(.)
15	Caller:	[[Al-
16	Host:	[[But you had no idea.
17	Caller:	No I- well I['m being honest.]
18	Host:	[And you came to a] con-=
19	Caller:	=[You don't] know ei:[ther.
20	Host:	[You had- yi] [You came to a conclusion
21		wuthahdenny- without any idea and without
22		even taking it into consideration.

The argument here is carried on not just in terms of competing positions, but also in terms of agents responsible for stating those positions. As M. H. Goodwin (1990) has noted in this regard: "Opposition can thus call into question not only what has been said but also the general competence of someone who would produce such talk" (p. 149).

In summary, we can see that it is possible for arguments on talk radio to shift relatively freely between mitigated and aggravated opposition formats. On this dimension, therefore, the arguments are at least formally "conversational" in character.

Shifts in Footing

Again, as in conversation, opposition turns on talk radio characteristically are directly addressed. This contrasts with the indirect address forms and implicit accusations found in more formal settings. But whereas hosts may engage as freely as callers in outright accusation, blame ascription, negation, and so on, we also find instances in which they use a particular technique—the "footing" shift—to modify the way in which a disagreement is couched. Goffman's (1981) notion of footing referred to the different ways in which a speaker can claim (or disclaim) personal responsibility for the words he or she is uttering. Clayman (1992) has shown how news interviewers, who work under a constraint of formal "neutrality," may manipulate their footing so as to put forward critical points to the interviewee while avoiding claiming any personal affiliation with those points. In this way, the interviewer presents him or herself as the proxy for the views of an absent third party.

Extract (10) shows the host using this technique, by which he is able to disclaim sole authorship for a position by attributing it to a third party. Here, the caller is complaining about the British government's proposal to increase the state pensions allowance. In response to her assertion in lines 1–2, the host begins to articulate the counterposition that "some pensioners in fact are doing rather better than they've ever done befo:re." Notice, however, the way he interrupts himself in the course of this turn (line 4) in order to redistribute authorship of that position, attributing responsibility for it to "some people including Nigel Lawson the Cha:ncellor":

(10) G:26.11.88:2:3

Caller: We're havin' a very very hard struggle at the
present moment.
(0.5)
Host: But what is your reply to the fact that- made
by some people including Nigel Lawson the
Cha:ncellor, .hh that some pensioners in fact
are doing rather better than they've ever done
befo:re.
(0.3)
Caller: Yes but it's the poorer ones that're feeling the
pin:ch,

The host here uses a "formal" strategy for presenting an alternative position, by means of which opposition between himself and the caller is moderated. In Clayman's (1992) analysis, such shifts in footing, when used by news interviewers, enable their producers to maintain a stance of official neutrality on an issue, while at the same time articulating a position that contrasts with that of the interviewee. As will become clearer shortly, hosts on talk radio certainly do not orient to a constraint for neutrality on their part. But while the footing shift device may not be functioning to protect anyone's neutrality in this instance, its use still serves to moderate opposition in the sense that the host thereby establishes a distance between himself and the counterposition he is articulating.

That form of moderated opposition can be contrasted with the next example, in which the host foregrounds opposition by such means as: (a) repeatedly responding to the caller's claims with overt expressions of disbelief (lines 7–8); and (b) undermining the caller's attempt to justify his claims ("I'm in the tra:de actually") with the overtly dismissive "I don't care what you're in" (line 18):

(11) H:2.2.89:12:2-3 ((The argument is about the problem of dogs fouling public places. The caller ostensibly intends to recommend a detergent product to combat dogs' natural propensity to "mark."))

1	Host:	This means that they never go in a different
2		pla:ce doesn't it.
3		(0.6)
4	Caller:	.thh Er the:y might go in: two or three places but,
5		(.) e::r, w-when they::, (.) u-deposit a er- er
6		lar:ge mess, it's usually[:,
7	Host:	[Mm. .h No I do:n't- I
8		don't believe that,=but you tell me about this-
9		this product? What is it ca:lled and what does
10		it [do?
11	Caller:	[Yes, (.) It is- it is tru:e, .h er:[m:,
12	Host:	[No I don't
13		believe it's tru:e because otherwise they'd go to
14		the same place every time.=Logic is not on your
15		si:de.
16		(.)
17	Caller:	(hn) E:r, well I'm in the tra:de ac(h)tually h=
18	Host:	=I don't care what you're in, logi[c is]not on=
19	Caller:	[°O:h°]
20	Host:	=your si:de.

Hosts, then, may relatively easily shift between opposition strategies that deemphasize their own responsibility for the contrary position being articulated, and those that actively highlight that responsibility. They may employ the mediating footing found in some formal settings, or the more direct, personal footing common in noninstitutional disputes.

Negotiation of Roles

All this suggests that on talk radio, the local negotiation of speaker roles is far freer than in formal types of institutional interaction. Hosts, although they may occupy the role of institutional agent vis-à-vis the caller, are not constrained in the range of argumentative actions open to them by the kind of turn-type and turn-order restrictions that operate in settings such as courtrooms and news interviews. It is not the case, for instance, that disputes on talk radio proceed by means of chains of question–answer sequences. We have seen that in local Action–Opposition sequences, hosts' turns may take a variety of forms, from questions to blame attributions to outright dismissals of callers' claims. And callers, in turn, may take up a range of local speaking roles, from responding to questions or challenges, to justifying assertions, through to countering hosts' accusations with reciprocal accusations of their own.

But as I suggested in chapter 1, that relative freedom of turn-exchange is embedded within quite a stable activity framework, in which at certain moments within the call, each participant orients to the accomplishment of specific tasks. Most significantly, the fact that the caller begins the call (and is expected to do so) by presenting an opinion on a chosen issue means that he or she is in a particular relationship to the host. Once the caller's opinion is on the line, the host takes on the role of respondent and potential challenger to that viewpoint.

At the same time, however, the host may refrain indefinitely from expressing his own opinion on the issue, thereby avoiding the possibility that the caller may reverse the roles and become the challenger. The way that calls are organized thus has the paradoxical upshot that the caller, although originally setting the agenda for the call, is on the defensive for most of the debate or dispute that follows. Or, at least, the host is in a better position to go on the offensive once the caller's opinion has been set on the line. The host has open to him a different set of interactional prerogatives from the caller, by virtue of the systematic arrangement of conduct within calls to the show. The basis and consequences of that central asymmetry will be the focus of attention in chapter 3.

In short, although there may be a considerable degree of freedom in the local negotiation of speaker roles within particular Action–Opposition sequences, superimposed on that is a more stable, institutionalized distribution of speaker identities which emerges from the very pattern of activities that the participants orient to on a call-by-call basis.

Rights to Express an Opinion

Hosts, unlike their counterpart institutional agents in formal settings, do not orient to any constraint that leads them to refrain from expressing personal opinions. Although they *may* refrain from overtly expressing an opinion in order to focus on producing piecemeal challenges to the caller's opinion (an option not open to the caller because he or she must have expressed an opinion at the start of the call), this does not mean that hosts adopt a stance of neutrality with regard to issues being discussed. At some point during most calls, hosts elect to express their personal opinions, and indeed use those opinions to build positions that directly vie with those of callers.

This is aptly illustrated by the following extract, in which the caller has been complaining about "people who object" to the apartheid regime in South Africa, but who in the caller's view do not have the courage of their convictions:

(12) H:23.1.89:10:1-2

1	Caller:	But you see, when you a:sk them the question, would
2		they like- democracy:, erm- (.) universal
3		franchi:se one ma:n one vote, tomorrow, (.) °.hhh°
4		(0.2) they a:ll seem to shift on their feet
5		they're not su:re. .hhh Because of course u-j-d
6		en:d up in chaos y'cou[ldn' do=it y'd aff t'ave a]
7	Host:	[Well n-ay a- v- d- a:sk m]=
8	Caller:	=tra:nsiti[onal period,]
9	Host:	[Ask m- Ask m]e: that question and see
10		what happen:s.
11	Caller:	Well I mean I- (.) u-w- I know 'ow perverse you are
12		Bri[an.=All ri:ght,]
13	Host:	[No=no not pe] not perverse at a[:ll.
14	Caller:	[A'right I'll
15		a:sk you the question=Would you like to see it
16		no:w=today=this a:fternoon.
17	Host:	.ph N:O:.
18		(0.8)
19	Caller:	R:i:ght. [(Now I mean 'at's) ri:ght so then you-]
20	Host:	[Na- neh- na-'nat's not- that's not sh]
21	Host:	=No: an' I'll- an' I'll tell you why. That's not
22		shifting edgily around the- the argument, it's
23		very very simple.=Because you can't cha:nge
24		anything overnight, .hhh and it's very f:oolish in
25		most cases, to do i[t.
26	Caller:	[You ca:n with a
27		v[ote Brian,
28	Host:	[Whatchu- notchu-
29		(.)
30	Host:	n[N-o you (d)-
31	Caller:	[Yes you ca-:n with a vo:te.
32		(.)
33	Host:	Na(d)- you ca:n't,
34		(.)
35	Caller:	[[If you 'ave a plebisc[i:te, you can ch]a:nge=
36	Host:	[[e:r yi [No you can make a]
37	Caller:	=things a:fter the plebiscite. [Ca:n't you.
38	Host:	[You can: ma:ke a
39		dec:ision, (0.3) but to actually: (0.3) carry that
40		ou:t overnight cannot be do:ne.

Throughout this extract the host emphasizes the partisan nature of his orientation toward the agenda introduced by the caller. In lines 9–10, his instruction to the caller to ask him the question and "see what happen:s" powerfully conveys that the host intends to take up a particular position upon being asked the question. Given that the caller has just described how "people who object" to the apartheid regime in South Africa "shift on their feet" when asked a straight question about whether they would like to see change (lines 1–5), what the host also conveys here, it seems, is that he is most definitely *not* going to shift on his feet when the question comes. His actual response, the emphatic "N:O:" in line 17, not only expresses his personal opinion, but also embodies the host's avoidance of "shifting on his feet," and is additionally partisan in that he thereby aligns himself with the category of "people who object" to the South African regime.

The point of view behind that simple "N:O:" is explicated in the sequence that follows. Here, we find the host electing to offer a justification for his position, and in fact overriding some talk of the caller's in order to do so (lines 20–25). After this, the caller begins to argue with that position (line 26), and there begins a burst of Action–Opposition sequences involving inversion ("Yes you can," "No you can't") which, again, are reminiscent of the conversational extracts discussed earlier.

In summary, disputes on talk radio are distinctive in a number of respects. First of all, talk radio is an institutional setting that does not involve strict institutionalized constraints on turn-order and turn-type. But although that is the case, institutional features are woven in and out of the interaction in terms of the activity patterns that characterize calls and the footing shifts that occur within them. Again, as in conversation, but unlike most other types of institutional interaction, opposition on talk radio may not only take mitigated forms but may equally be aggravated and highly confrontational. Finally, the confrontational character of the disputes is often linked to the fact that hosts, unlike most other institutional agents, are free to express their own opinions on issues. Moreover, as we will see in chapter 3, the fact that they can also refrain from expressing their view indefinitely is itself connected to the specialized nature of confrontation talk on talk radio.

CONCLUSION

These observations on the management of arguments on talk radio are intended to show something of the way in which those arguments exhibit the quasi-conversational forms that Drew and Heritage (1992) propose are characteristic of nonformal types of institutional interaction. The term *quasi-conversational* is of course not meant to imply that there are no discernible, systematic differences at all between turn-taking procedures in these settings and those characteristic of conversation. The point rather relates specifically to the comparative perspective adopted within conversation analysis: "When considered in turn-taking terms at least, the boundaries between these forms of institutional talk and ordinary conversation can appear permeable and uncertain" (p. 28).

We have seen some of that permeability and uncertainty here. But I have also suggested that particular kinds of asymmetry emerge in disputes between hosts and callers, which are somehow related to distinctive institutional features of the talk. In the next chapter, bearing the model of arguments as Action–Opposition sequences in mind, I turn to look more closely at some of these asymmetries, tracing their basis by relating together the Action–Opposition model and the routine activity-pattern of calls.

3 Arguments, Agendas, and Asymmetries

Talk radio represents a public context in which private citizens can articulate their opinions on social issues. In different shows, the space allotted to callers to put forward their views is mapped out in different ways. For instance, some shows expressly address themselves to one issue per broadcast, and the caller's role is to have a say on that issue while the host acts as a moderator, relating contributions together and drawing out differences and similarities between them.[1] But in open-line shows like the *Brian Hayes Programme,* callers select their own issue to talk about, and they are given the floor at the beginning of calls in order to introduce their issue and express an opinion on it. In this sense open-line talk radio shows enable callers to set the agenda for a discussion with the host.

However, the agenda is not something that is fixed; nor is it established from one perspective only. Particularly when argument is in the air, the agenda itself can become the contested arena for disputes focusing on what is "relevantly sayable." This leads to a kind of paradox in talk radio disputes. Although it may seem that the caller, in setting the agenda for the call, is in a position of control over what might count as an acceptable or relevant contribution to their topic, in fact it is the host who tends to end up in that position, and it is the host who has open to him a more powerful set of argumentative resources. So, although introducing an agenda is the caller's prerogative on talk radio, this leads to a situation in which the argumentative

[1]An example of this in British broadcasting is the BBC's weekly show *Call Nick Ross.*

initiative can rest with the host, and the caller can relatively easily be put on the defensive. In this chapter, I will describe just how that situation comes about. In doing so, I will examine the use of some argumentative resources that are unequally available to hosts and callers.

In chapter 2, I proposed that in order to understand the management of disputes in institutional settings, we need to focus squarely on the types of Action–Opposition sequences, and the particular forms of oppositional move, that characterize such disputes. Here I begin to look at asymmetrical and institutional features of arguments on talk radio by focusing on the resources available to hosts to construct opposition to callers' agenda-setting introductions. In the process, I show how an asymmetrical distribution of oppositional resources is linked to the basic activity-pattern of calls. Building on some remarks by Sacks (1992), I suggest that a generic feature of argument sequences is the difference between "going first" and "going second" with one's views on an arguable issue. This introduces a new angle on the Action–Opposition sequence model. First and second positions can involve quite different kinds of resources, and in an important sense, disputants who get to go second are in a more powerful position than those who go first. I show that the activity-pattern of calls places callers in first position—they are required to begin by stating their view on an issue. Hosts thus have available a set of argumentative resources that are not available in the same way to callers. In this sense, the present chapter begins to address the link between power in discourse and the local sequential organization of interaction within individual calls.

TAKING UP A POSITION

Before beginning to look at the resources available to hosts to react to, and construct opposition to, callers' opinions, it is important to say something about the patterned ways in which callers take up their positions in the first place.

I mentioned in chapter 1 that calls' openings are structured in a particular way. In the first phase, callers are announced by the host and then the two participants exchange greetings. Following the greeting, callers move into the second phase of the call by introducing the topic they want to address. In this transition, callers can be seen to take up incumbency in their role of opinion-producer in their very first turns on the air. The following set of extracts illustrates how callers make the transition between greetings and topic-introduction relatively unproblematically:

(1) H:23.1.89:2:1

Host: Bob is calling from Ilford. Good morning.
Caller: .hh Good morning Brian. (0.4) .hh What I'm phoning
up is about the cricket. . .

(2) H:30.11.88:10:1

Host: Mill Hill:: i:s where Belinda calls from. Good
morning.
Caller: Good morning Brian. .hh Erm, re the Sunday
o:pening I'm just phoning from the point of
vie:w, .hh as a:n assistant. . .

(3) H:21.11.88:11:1

Host: On to Philip in Camden Town. Good morning.
Caller: Yeh guh morning Brian. Erm (.) Really what I
wanted to say was that I'm fascinated by watching
these telethons by the anuh- amount'v
contradictions that're thrown up by them. . .

In each case here, the topic is overtly nominated as the reason for the call: for instance, in (1), "What I'm phoning up is about the cricket"; in (2) "re the Sunday o:pening"; or in (3), "Really what I wanted to say was that I'm fascinated by watching these telethons. . . ." There is also a sense in which those topics get introduced not just as topics but as *issues*. This is done by referring to them using the definite article (e.g., "the cricket," "the Sunday o:pening"). Using this form of reference, callers can provide their topics with a sense of being generally recognizable. As Clark and Haviland (1977) observed, to describe a topic with the prefix "the" is to invoke some degree of shared knowledge between speaker and recipient(s). This way of introducing topics thus constructs them as given themes in the public domain, and the fact that something is recognizably in the public domain is a significant way in which it can be construed as an issue.

The way in which callers orient to the status of their topics as public issues is also illustrated by the fact that callers do not phone in about personal or private problems and complaints, not, at least, unless these can be explicitly related to an identifiable public concern. For instance, in the following extract the caller begins by stating that "We've got a real problem he:re"; but that problem is linked to the public issue of "dogs fouling our footways":

(4) H:2.2.89:4:1

Host: And good morning to Ma:ndy from Ruislip. Good
morni[ng.
Caller: [Good mor:ning Brian. .hhh We've got a real
problem he:re with dogs fouling our footway,

A further point to make about these topic introductions is that by overtly marking them, in various ways, as "what the call will be about," callers also propose that something more, some further talk on the issue, is forthcoming. That further talk tends to be of a particular kind. Callers do not just introduce an agenda; they further frame that agenda by taking up a position on the issue they have selected. In other words, these initial turns take the form of what Schiffrin (1985) described as "rhetorical arguments": Multisentence monologues in which a speaker makes a case for a disputable position. The following set of extracts provides a sense of the kind of tendentious talk that routinely occurs in these turns.

In extract (5), the caller takes up a position on the issue she introduces as her reason for calling: "Diana's [the Princess of Wales'] visit to America." Note that while the topic itself is introduced in a neutral fashion (as it is in 1: "What I"m phoning up is about the cricket," and in 2: "re the Sunday o:pening,") the caller's subsequent talk makes it clear that she treats this as a controversial issue about hypocrisy among society's wealthier classes:

(5) H:2.2.89:3:1

Host: It's Ka:y next from: Islington:, good morning.
Caller: Yes guh morning. Um:: (.) I: want to talk about
thee- thee report on L.B.C this morning about
Diana's visi:t to::, America:? h[.hh
Host: [The Princess
of Wa:les.
(.)
Caller: Princess of Wa:les, yah. .hh E::r th- her stay
in a thou:sand pou:nds a night hotel plus V.A.T::,
an' on her schedule she's visiting a home- p-
place for the homeless. .hhh A:nd there's going
to be a ba:::ll, .hh where they're uh- the
Americans are clamoring for tickets at a thou:sand
pounds a ni- er th- a thou:sand pounds each,=
Host: =[Mm hm,]
Caller: [I: th]ink it's obsce:ne.
Host: .pt Which:, part is obsce:ne.

In her account of rhetorical arguments, Schiffrin (1985) notes that they tend to consist of two types of component: "descriptions," and "assessments" or evaluations.[2] We can see both these types of component in this extract. After

[2]This distinction between descriptive and evaluative talk is a slippery one. As Pomerantz (1984b) has shown, when a speaker engages in descriptive talk of any kind, he or she unavoidably displays in the details of the description a stance taken toward the description's accuracy, truthfulness, or completeness. For instance, a description can be offered as a true or certain account of "the facts," or it can be constructed to display a degree of skepticism or doubt about its own veracity. Or a speaker may offer a description in the guise of a "mere report," in which information is provided only "as known" to the speaker. In short, an implicit evaluative element is incorporated in descriptive talk of any sort. Schiffrin (1985), however, is referring to components in arguments in which a speaker articulates an evaluative stance on the issue *explicitly,* for instance through the use of what Heritage and Greatbatch (1986) described as "position-taking" devices, such as "I: think it's obsce:ne." On this level, the distinction seems sustainable.

introducing her topic, the caller describes some details about the Princess' visit. The way she builds this description is clearly designed to convey a sense of hypocrisy on the part of the Princess. This is done by contrasting the price of the hotel suite (line 9) and of tickets for a ball (line 14) with the fact that she intends to "visit a . . . place for the homeless." The stance that is implied by this juxtaposition is then taken up explicitly with an assessment: "I: think it's obsce:ne" (line 16).

This assessment seems to be recognized by the host as a possible completion of the caller's argument. Immediately after it, he embarks on his response. Schiffrin (1985) observes that assessments, although they may freely occur within an argument, tend strongly to occur at the boundaries of argument-making turns (i.e., at the beginning and/or the end). In fact, the shift from description to assessment is a characteristic way that speakers have of signaling a move toward closure of many kinds of extended turn, such as those in which a story has been told (Jefferson, 1978; Labov, 1972; Labov & Waletsky, 1967) or a complaint made (Drew & Holt, 1988); whereas Heritage and Greatbatch (1986) focused on overt evaluations such as "I think it's obscene" as an applause-elicitation device in political speeches.[3]

The role of position-taking evaluations as "boundary-markers" in turns where a speaker makes an argument has been noted in a slightly different way by van Eemeren et al. (1987) when they describe:

> the two ways in which a speaker can give a verbal presentation of the relationship between an opinion and one or more arguments:
>
> (1) He first gives a number of arguments and then draws a conclusion (opinion);
>
> (2) He advances a thesis (opinion) and then supports it by one or more arguments.
>
> In the first instance, then, the arguments precede the opinion and we speak of a progressive presentation; in the second, the arguments follow the opinion and we speak of a retrogressive presentation. (p. 22)

If the extract we have just examined takes the first of these patterns, with the caller's opinion coming at the end, the following extract illustrates that callers may also use the second pattern, in which an opinion is presented first:

(6) H:21.11.88:6:1

1	Host:	Kath calling from Clapham now good morning.
2	Caller:	Good morning Brian. Erm: I (li-) I also agree
3		that thee .hh telethons a:re a form of
4		psychological blackmail no:w. (.) .hhh Be:cause

[3]For a detailed consideration of the functions of assessments in conversation generally, see C. Goodwin and M. H. Goodwin (1992).

5 the majority of people I think do know that
6 charities exist, .hh we all have our own
7 charities that we contribute to:, (.) .h we do
8 not have open ended pockets where we can keep on
9 doing this. .hh And to sa:y because you have a
10 credit car::d, .hh you just salve your conscience
11 by paying- sending in your number:, .phh I'm
12 sorry but I: think that's making people, (.)
13 appear very erm (.) la:zy.=
14 Host: =Well it's certainly not blackmail,

Here the caller does not begin with a neutral introduction, but with an evaluation (lines 2–4). She then goes on to present arguments to justify that position, marking the justification through the use of the conjunction, "Because" (line 4). However, we might note that she in fact ends with another assessment (lines 12–13), after which, again, the host reacts.

The caller in the next extract also uses a version of the second strategy. Beginning with an evaluative formulation, in which he ironically describes himself as "fascinated by watching these telethons," he goes on to justify his own negative stance on the issue, by first citing a favorable argument made by "people who support" telethons; then pointing to a way in which he thinks that argument can be faulted. Once more, the host's reaction to the argument comes after the caller has produced an assessment of the state of "childcare facilities" that he has described: "in fa:ct it's getting wor::se."

(7) H:21.11.88:11:1 ((Extension of Extract 3))
1 Host: On to Philip in Camden Town. Good morning.
2 Caller: Yeh guh morning Brian. Erm (.) Really what I
3 wanted to say was that I'm fascinated by watching
4 these telethons by the anuh- amount'v
5 contradictions that're thrown up by them. .hh I
6 mean one of the arguments that're made by people
7 who support them is that the state can't sort of
8 fill a bottomless pit, of need but when you
9 look at er the childcare facilities in this
10 country:, .hh we're very very low, (.) i-on the
11 league table in Europe of (.) you know if you
12 try to get a child into a nursery it's very
13 difficult in this country. .hh An' in fa:ct it's
14 getting wor::se.
15 Host: What's that got to do with it.

In various ways, then, callers' first turns are designed not only to express an opinion, but also to provide arguments to justify the position that is taken up. Calls are organized so that an institutional space is provided at the outset in which the caller may do this. For the most part, callers straightforwardly orient to their role of opinion-producer by going straight from greeting the host to introducing their topic and making their argument. As the following extract illustrates, however, it is also the case that the host expects that callers should begin calls in this way:

(8) H:2.2.89:7:1

Host:	Jo:hn next.
	(.)
Caller:	He- Hello?
Host:	Hello John in: Marylebone.
Caller:	Er, hello er, your- your people didn't give me
	any wa:rning er, (.) Okay. [.h
Host:	[Well I said hello:
	you're John now that was the warning now what
	d'you have to say.
Caller:	Right. Erm, (.) i:t's about the dogs. . .

Here, the host's first turn does not take the customary form of [Name + Town + Greeting] but merely names the caller. Perhaps as a result of this, the caller's first "Hello?" (line 3) is tentative: it comes after a brief pause and has a questioning intonation. The host responds by providing a second initial turn, this time incorporating the more usual three components (line 4). At this stage, then, from the host's point of view the caller has received not one but two introductions, and hence has been provided with two opportunities to move into introducing his topic. Yet the caller's next move is still not to introduce a topic, but to provide an account for his failure to do so in his previous turn (lines 5–6). The host's palpably irritated response (lines 7–9) illustrates his own orientation to the expectation that callers should treat his opening turn not just as an announcement and a greeting, but also as a cue to introduce their topic and have their say.

The opening phases of calls, then, are organized around a mutual expectation that it is the caller rather than the host who is primarily responsible for setting the agenda that will be addressed. But as I want to show now, there is a paradoxical upshot to this. Although the caller sets the initial agenda for each call, the arguments which ensue are ones in which the host is disagreeing with, challenging, or being skeptical of the caller's remarks. This means that the host can find it relatively easy to go on the offensive in disputes, whereas the caller finds him or herself in a defensive position with regard to the agenda they began by introducing.

This asymmetry is an outcome of the way in which not only calls but also arguments themselves are sequentially organized. Viewing arguments as constructed out of Action–Opposition sequences, as I described in chapter 2, we can see that the structure of calls, in which callers begin by setting out their position, situates the caller's talk as a first move in a possible Action–Opposition sequence. In other words, it is the host who has the "first opportunity for opposition" within each call.[4] This first opportunity for opposition turns out to be a powerful argumentative resource, which is not only linked to a particular kind of asymmetry between hosts and callers, but also has consequences for the shape and trajectory of disputes in the talk radio setting.

FIRST AND SECOND POSITIONS IN ARGUMENTS

The first opportunity for opposition is linked to a broader asymmetry in the organization of arguments, which works at the level of arguing for and against particular positions. I remarked in the last chapter that Action–Opposition sequences have the potential to emerge at any point in interaction. As Maynard (1985) writes, "any utterance or action may contain objectionable features and may become part of a dispute" (p. 3). This means that it is not necessary for someone to be actually engaged in putting forward an opinion on a controversial issue for an argument to occur. However, on many occasions—among them, calls to the open-line talk radio show—participants do indeed engage in arguing for and against positions on issues. And in this kind of activity, there are consequential differences between going first and going second with one's opinion, where going second actually means having the *first* opportunity for opposition.

The asymmetry between first and second positions in arguments was first remarked on by Sacks in one of his lectures on conversation (1992, Vol. 2, pp. 340–347). Sacks proposed that those who go first are in a weaker position than those who get to go second, because, quite simply, the latter can argue with the former's position simply by taking it apart. Going first means having to set your opinion on the line, whereas going second means being able to argue merely by challenging your opponent to expand on or account for his or her claims.

In many situations, first and second positions are open to strategic competition between participants. In such situations we can find speakers using systematic means to try and avoid first position, or to try and prompt or maneuver another into taking first position. For instance, Sacks discusses the following fragment of data:

(9) GTS [From a conversation among teenagers]
1 Jim: Isn't the New Pike de<u>press</u>ing?

---

[4]Callers' first turns may of course be "oppositional" in the sense of opposing something that was said previously in the broadcast. But the relevant point for my purposes is that within each individual encounter between the host and a caller, and hence within each new broadcast argument, it is the host who has the first opportunity to construct opposition to the words or actions of his interlocutor.

2 Mike: hhh The Pike?
3 Jim: Yeah. Oh the place is disgusting. Any day of the
4 week.

In line 1, Jim indicates a position on the "New Pike," a local amusement park. I say he "indicates" a position because, as Sacks remarks, "To say 'Isn't the New Pike depressing?' is sequentially altogether different than saying 'God the New Pike is depressing'" (1992, Vol. 2, p. 345). Although both formulations make the speaker's own opinion clear, the version used by Jim merely implies his opinion, and invites Mike's agreement. The turn is built to prefer agreement, in the sense outlined in chapter 2.

In the next turn, however, Mike neither agrees nor disagrees with Jim. Rather, he produces a turn which on one level looks like an "understanding check": a turn in which he initiates repair on Jim's prior turn, perhaps because he isn't sure he properly heard what Jim said. But there are features of Mike's turn that go against such an interpretation. For instance, he doesn't say, "The what?"—which would be a straightforward way of indicating a possible mishearing or misunderstanding (Schegloff, Jefferson, & Sacks, 1977). Neither does he repeat Jim's naming of the place in full ("The New Pike?"), which again might suggest a difficulty in locating the referent in his own stock of knowledge (Clark & Schaefer, 1989). Rather, he "re-references" the amusement park, calling it "The Pike," an abbreviation which in fact suggests his familiarity with it. Finally, Jim himself exhibits in his next turn that he does not take Mike's utterance to be initiating repair, by carrying on with and expanding his assessment (lines 3–4) instead of repairing his first turn by saying, for example, "Yeah. You know, the amusement park?"

Instead of an understanding check, Mike's turn can be treated as a move in an incipient argument: a maneuver by which the floor is thrown back to Jim with an invitation to go on and develop his position on the ways in which the New Pike is in fact depressing. It is a maneuver that seeks to place Mike in second position with respect to Jim's opinion of the Pike. If he can succeed in maneuvering Jim into first position, Mike would then be in a position to attack Jim's view by using what Jim said as a resource for disagreeing, rather than immediately focusing on building a defense for his own alternative position.

This is precisely what happens as the conversation proceeds. Jim goes on to elaborate on his view of the Pike, which then places Mike in a position to attack that view merely by undermining its weaknesses, rather than arguing for a particular counterposition:

(10) GTS
1 Jim: But you go down- dow- down to the New Pike there's
2 a buncha people, oh:: an' they're old, an' they're
3 pretending they're having fun, but they're really
4 not.

Mike: How can you tell. Hm?
Jim: They're- they're tryina make a living, but the place is on the decline, 's like a degenerate place. . .

In line 5 here, Mike takes up a critical stance vis-à-vis Jim's argument, not by putting forward a counterposition, but by undermining Jim's competence to make the claims he is making. This is done by using "How can you tell?" to challenge Jim's grounds for the claim that people at the New Pike are "really not" having fun. This turn does not give Jim much in the way of resources that will allow him to take up the offensive and challenge Mike. Rather, his options are either to account for how he can tell, or to attempt to change tack.

It is this situation which is at the root of the asymmetry between first and second positions in argument. While first position arguers are required to build a defense for their stance, those in second position are able to choose if and when they will set out their own argument, as opposed to simply attacking the other's.

Now as I have already suggested, on talk radio this asymmetry is one that is built into the overall structure of calls. Callers are expected to go first with their line, whereas the host systematically gets to go second, and thus to contest the caller's line by picking at its weaknesses. The fact that hosts systematically have the first opportunity for opposition within calls opens to them a collection of argumentative resources that are not available in the same way to callers. In the following section, I will explore some of the uses and consequences of these second position resources, concentrating on episodes in which the contest is about the dispute's agenda itself.

AGENDA CONTESTS

Validity Challenges

One of the things that argument may be about is the struggle between participants over what can and cannot legitimately be said in a dispute: in other words, defining the boundaries of the dispute's agenda. I have already remarked that on talk radio, calls' agendas have an interesting status. Whereas it is the role of the caller to set up an agenda for discussion, that agenda is not something that the caller necessarily maintains subsequent control of. By being in second position, the host is able to challenge the agenda-relatedness of the caller's remarks: to question whether what the caller says is actually relevant within the terms of his or her own agenda.

One way in which this may be done is through the use of what I will call "validity challenges." Validity challenges are a class of utterances, including "So?" and "What's that got to do with it?" which oppose a claim on the grounds of its relevance to the matter in question. However, although they oppose the claim's validity, such turns need not make clear precisely on what terms its relevance is being challenged. They may function purely as second position moves by which the first speaker is required to expand on or account for the challenged claim.

(11) H:21.11.88:6:1

1	Caller:	I: have got three appeals letters here this week.
2		(0.4) All a:skin' for donations. (0.2) .hh Two:
3		from tho:se that I: always contribute to
4		anywa:y,
5	Host:	Yes?
6	Caller:	.hh But I expect to get a lot mo:re.
7	Host:	So?
8	Caller:	.h Now the point is there is a limi[t to ( )
9	Host:	[What's that got
10		to do- what's that got to do with telethons though.
11	Caller:	hh Because telethons. . . ((Continues))

The caller here is complaining about the number of mailed requests for charitable donations she receives. In line 7 the host responds by saying "So?" As an argumentative move, this turn achieves two things. First, it challenges the validity or relevance of the caller's complaint within the terms of her own agenda, which is that telethons (and also, it seems, charity mail) represent a form of "psychological blackmail" (the extract comes from the same call as extract [6], shown previously). Secondly, because it stands alone as a complete turn, "So?" requires the caller to take the floor again and *account* for the relevance of her remark.

In this second sense, the use of "So?" as a validity challenge is somewhat different to an alternative argumentative use of the same item, in the context of what M. H. Goodwin (1990), studying children's arguments, has termed "disclaimers." A disclaimer is "an action that denies the *relevance* of a prior action without disagreeing with it. . . . Frequently turns containing disclaimers have distinctive prefaces. Thus terms such as "so," "I don't care" and "I know" can be used to begin turns containing reasons why current speaker considers prior speaker's talk to be of no consequence" (p. 153).

For example:

(12) Goodwin, 1990

1	Benita:	I'm eight and a half. I'm almost nine.
2→	Larry:	So, my brother older than you.

(13) Goodwin, 1990

1	Kerry:	Why you wanna bother with him. He's smaller than
2		you.
3→	Earl:	So, he keep mouthing off with me.

The difference here is that "so" is a preface to a further component in the second speaker's turn, which either (a) offers a counter to the first speaker's claim (in [12]), or (b) provides a reason for the action first speaker has complained about (in [13]). In these cases, as Goodwin notes, "so" seems to do the work of denying the importance of the prior action.

By contrast, when "So" stands on its own in a turn, as in extract (11), it challenges the relevance of the prior speaker's claim in both a more fundamental and a more oppositional sense. In the cases cited by Goodwin, "so" prefaces can be used to *accept,* while denying the importance of, a prior claim, complaint, or threat. Second speakers themselves then go on to provide grounds for its unimportance or irrelevance. The freestanding "So?" used by the host in extract (11), however, stands more clearly in opposition to the caller's claims, and sets up a different relationship between the participants in which it is the first speaker rather than the second who should, in a next turn, account for the validity of what has just been said.

In this sense, "So?" functions in a similar way to the other validity challenge used in extract (11), the host's "What's that got to do with telethons" (line 10). In the same way that the caller responds to the first challenge by formulating the point of her remarks (line 8), at this second challenge she responds by providing a reason for her claims (line 11). This is illustrated again in the call from which extract (7) was taken:

(14) H:21.11.88:11:1

Caller: When you look at e:r the childcare facilities in
this country, .hh we're very very low, (.) i-on the
league table in Europe of (.) you know if you
try to get a child into a nursery it's very
difficult in this country. .hh An' in fa:ct it's
getting wor::se.
Host: What's that got to do with it.
Caller: .phh Well I think whu- what 'at's gotta d- do with
it is. . . ((Continues))

Again, the host's validity challenge (line 7) situates the caller in a position of providing an account for the relevance of his remarks within the terms of the agenda which he himself has introduced.

Validity challenges, then, represent one resource by which the host can rapidly put callers on the defensive about their own agenda. By challenging the agenda-relevance of callers' remarks, the host may effectively "hijack" strategic control over the field of relevancies locally at work within a dispute.

Formulating

Another way in which the host may attempt to establish control over the agenda is by selectively "formulating" the gist or upshot of the caller's remarks. Heritage (1985) described the practice of formulating as: "summarizing, glossing, or developing the gist of an informant's earlier statements. Although it is relatively rare in conversation, it is common in institutionalized, audience-directed interaction" (e.g., settings such as courtrooms, classrooms and news interviews; p. 100).

Heritage (1985) also notes that in these institutional settings, formulating "is most commonly undertaken by questioners" (p. 100). This accords with the common finding in studies of institutional discourse that "[i]nstitutional incumbents (doctors, teachers, interviewers, family social workers, etc.) may strategically direct the talk through such means as their capacity to change topics and their selective formulations, in their 'next questions,' of the salient points in the prior answers" (Drew & Heritage, 1992, p. 49).[5]

On talk radio, formulations can be used both in a relatively benign, summarizing role, and also as argumentative moves in which the host uses the formulation to take issue with the caller's claims. The following extract illustrates the first, benign use of the formulation:

(15) G:26.11:88:2

Caller: It- it is it's really it is the poor, the poorer
pensioners that've had it taken away from them.
(0.4) Because of this er money that's been e:r the
means allowance money.
Host: So you don't think the government's being all that
marvellous and generous about th[is.
Caller: [I: think they're
dis::gusting.
Host: Uh [thank-]
Caller: [I real]ly do.
Host: Thank you Margaret. . .

In lines 5–6, the host glosses the caller's stance in a single sentence. This works as a "cooperative" formulation (Heritage, 1985), offering the caller a version of her position to which she can assent. As Heritage and Watson (1979) have pointed out, formulations such as this, in cooperatively summarizing a discussion, can often work as moves toward bringing discussions to a close. And this is what happens here, as the host uses the caller's emphatic agreement with his formulation as a cue to close the call.

The next excerpt, however, shows the more argumentative use of formulations. The host here uses two strategically linked proposals of upshot to contentiously reconstruct the position being advanced by the caller. The caller

[5]These themes have been most evident in studies of doctor–patient interaction, notably Fisher and Todd (1987), Silverman (1987), and Davis (1988).

has criticized the "contradictions" of telethons (recall extract [3], earlier), claiming that their rhetoric of concern in fact promotes a passive altruism which exacerbates the "separateness" between donors and recipients. He goes on:

(16) H:21.11.88:11:3

1	Caller:	. . .but e:r, I- I think we should be working at
2		breaking down that separateness I [think]these
3	Host:	[Ho:w?]
4		(.)
5	Caller:	these telethons actually increase it.
6	Host:	Well, what you're saying is that charity does.
7	Caller:	.h Charity do::es, ye[::s I mean-]
8	Host:	[Okay we- so you]'re (.) so
9		you're going back to that original argument we
10		shouldn't have charity.
11	Caller:	Well, no I um: I wouldn't go that fa:r, what I
12		would like to [see is-
13	Host:	[Well how far are you going then.
14	Caller:	Well I: would- What I would like to see is. . .

In line 6, the host inferentially elaborates the caller's argument, by proposing that its field of relevance in fact embraces charities in general and not just telethons as one sort of charitable endeavor. And although the caller has not made any such generalization himself, he assents to this in the next turn. It appears, then, that the formulation here is being used in the same cooperative manner as in the previous extract.

However, it turns out that the caller, by agreeing, provides the host with a resource for contentiously reformulating the agenda in play here. By linking a second formulation to the first, this time describing the upshot of the caller's position, it is proposed that the caller is going back to an argument which the host had with a previous caller, whose view had been that "we shouldn't have charity" (lines 8–10).

The caller in fact rejects this further formulation (line 11). But the significant point is this: The host is able to use the fact that the call is in some sense about what the caller thinks about an issue to construct an argument without putting himself in the position of having to defend his own view. By relying on his ability to formulate the gist or upshot of the caller's remarks, the host can issue challenges over some underlying agenda at work in the caller's contribution.

It is in this sense that the agenda contests that occur within calls reveal significant aspects of the play of power in the conduct of talk radio disputes. The fact that callers must begin by setting an agenda means that argumentative resources are distributed asymmetrically between host and callers. The host is able to build opposition using second position resources such as validity challenges and formulations. The characteristic feature of these resources is that they require callers to defend or account for their claims, while enabling hosts to argue without constructing a defense for an alternative view. At the same time, as long as the host refrains from setting out his own position, such second position resources are not available to the caller. Distinctive interactional prerogatives are thereby available to the host, by which he can exert a degree of control over the boundaries of an agenda ostensibly set by the caller.

TURNING THE TABLES

The implication so far has been that the way calls are set up provides the host with a natural incumbency in second position. This does not mean, however, that callers are incapable of offering resistance to the host's challenges. One way of doing this is to adopt the use of second position resources on their own part. But, as I have just suggested, particular sequential environments are necessary for this. In particular, the host must have moved or been maneuvered into adopting first position (that is, indicating a position in his own right). The host is able to choose when, or if, he will express his own view on the caller's issue: Technically, he is able to conduct a whole call simply by challenging and demanding justifications for the caller's claims. This is very rare, however, and once the host has abandoned second position, that position then becomes available for the caller.

Extract (17), taken from the "Princess of Wales" call, shows how a caller may succeed in turning the tables in this way. As we will see, in this case the tables are turned only briefly because the host subsequently adopts a strategy for reestablishing himself in second position:

(17) H:2.2.89:3:3

```
Caller:   But I still think a thousand pounds a night at a
          hotel:, .hhh a:nd the fact that she's going on to
          visit homeless peop[le,
Host:                        [Where should sh- Where should
          she be staying in New York.
          (0.2)
Caller:   We:ll u-th- at a cheaper place I don't think the
          money-=.h WE'RE paying that money for her to stay
          there and I think it's ob°scene.
Host:     Well we're not actually paying the[e the the money,
Caller:                                     [Well   who:'s
          paying for it.
Host:     Well thee:: e:rm I imagine the the:r the money the
```

Royal Family has .h er is paying for it, .h or
indeed it may be paid for by somebody else, .h
erm but .h y'know if the Princess of Wales lives
in: (.) a palace in this country, w-w-why do
you think she should not live in something which is
(.) comparable, .hh when she's visiting New York?
Caller: Well I should think that she could find something
comparable that- that- or- e-it could be found
for her that doesn't cost that money.

One thing we can notice is the way the caller responds to the host's hostile questioning (which has been going on for some while) by attempting to suddenly shift the topical focus of her agenda (line 8). From the question of the price of the hotel suite, she shifts, by means of a self-interruption, to the perhaps more powerful issue of the ultimate responsibility of the taxpayer for footing the bill: ".h WE'RE paying that money for her to stay there."

The host's response to this, in line 10, is significant. By opposing the caller's assertion, he abandons his series of questioning challenges and instead asserts a position in his own right. It is this turn that allows the caller to move onto the offensive, and produce a challenge of her own which, in a way characteristic of the second position moves I have been discussing, requires the host to account for his assertion (lines 11–12).

At this stage, then, the local roles of challenger and defender of a position have been inverted. The host, from being in his customary challenger role, has suddenly been swung around into the role of defender. However, this inversion turns out to be only temporary. In the very next turn, the host manages to reestablish the prior state of affairs. He does this by not only responding to the caller's challenge, but also going on to produce a next challenge-bearing question of his own (lines 16–19). With this move, the host succeeds in doing two things. First, he reestablishes the agenda to which his earlier question, in the second turn of the extract, had been addressed and which the caller had attempted to shift away from. Secondly, he resituates the caller as the respondent to his challenging initiatives, rather than as the initiator of challenge-bearing moves herself.

The asymmetry between first and second positions is not, then, a monolithic, one-way feature of talk radio disputes. Although the organizational structure of calls situates callers in first position initially, they may subsequently find themselves with opportunities to move into the stronger second position. As extract (17) shows, the sequential space for this arises once the host has abandoned the second position strategy of issuing challenges and made an assertion in his own right. It is this move that enables the caller in turn to adopt second position. However, the extract also shows that there are strategies available for turning the tables *back* again, and this suggests that second position itself can become actively contested over a series of turns.

To illustrate this, finally, we can continue with the "Princess of Wales" call, and find that the caller subsequently adopts the host's strategy in order to retake the initiative in the argument. The following extract begins toward the end of extract (17):

(18) H:2.2.89:3:3

20	Caller:	Well I should think that she could find something
21		comparable that- that- or- e-it could be found
22		for her that doesn't cost that money. A[nd] you're=
23	Host:	[But]
24	Caller:	=only imagining that she's paying for herself you
25		don't know ei:ther do you.
26	Host:	E:rm, well. . .

The feature of interest here is in lines 22 and 24. In a way similar way to that of the host in the previous talk, the caller moves from providing a response to a challenge to issuing a question. This puts the host in the position of having to respond and further account for his own position that "she's paying for herself." In part, the basis for this second challenge lies in the host's long turn in lines 13–19 of extract (17), earlier, where he responded to the caller's first challenge. That is, the caller is not simply revisiting or revamping the earlier challenge, but developing a new line of attack that relies on the fact that the host's earlier response had been quite vague (see especially lines 13–15 of extract [17]).

In summary, although the call's initial stages situate the caller in first position and furnish the host with the power of second position, that asymmetry is not an unchanging feature of the context. The more powerful argumentative resources attached to second position may also become available to the caller, and callers who are determined and resourceful enough may challenge the host using second position tactics, even as the host himself attempts to readopt the more powerful position.

CONCLUSION

In this chapter, my principal focus has been the host's use of second position resources such as validity challenges and formulations, by which he may exert a degree of discursive power by contesting the agenda-relevance of the caller's talk. However, that discussion may have given the impression that only rarely does the host articulate his own point of view on the issue in question. This, of course, is not the case. At some stage in almost every call in my data corpus, the host begins to argue for a position, usually (but not always) one that is opposed to that of the caller.

My point has rather been to stress that there is an asymmetry between hosts and callers in terms of how and when their positions may be articulated. The caller is *required* to stake out a position at the beginning of the call, whereas the host may *choose* when he will stake out his own position. This chapter's focus has been on how that asymmetry is exploited by hosts through the practice of withholding their personal point of view in favor of issuing second position challenges that require the caller to defend the agenda-relevance of his or her remarks. I have suggested that this asymmetry and its exploitation can be seen as one basis for the power relationship between the participants on talk radio, where power is understood as expressed in discourse, through an unequal distribution and deployment of argumentative resources.

But clearly, hosts do not argue just by challenging the agenda-relevance of caller's statements. As we will see in chapter 4, there are other ways in which hosts can exploit the caller's own argument in building opposition and articulating their own positions. The discussion there will focus on one resource, which I call the "You say (X)" device, through which the host is able to engage in argument by turning callers' claims against themselves.

4 The Pursuit of Controversy

Talk radio is an institutionalized setting for what might be called "opinionated" talk, a setting in which arguments are a routine occurrence. But however routine the activity might be, the arguments that actually take place are entirely ad hoc. In this, talk radio is unlike many other institutional settings for dispute, such as courtroom examination (Drew, 1992) or broadcast news interviews (Greatbatch, 1988, 1992). In such settings, participants from both sides have a good idea beforehand what their argument will be about and may well have prepared their case in detail. On talk radio, on the other hand, arguments emerge locally out of the improvised opening statements that callers make at the beginning of calls.[1] The host has little idea of the possible contents of each caller's position prior to the production of these statements. Consequently, if he wants to build opposition in pursuit of the kind of controversial talk for which open-line talk radio shows are notorious, he will have to closely monitor the caller's account for possible arguables.

The device at the center of this chapter represents a major resource that the host draws on to construct such ad hoc arguments. One significant feature of it is that it enables the host to exhibit skepticism of the claims and as-

[1]The improvized nature of callers' opening arguments appears to be something that talk radio stations are concerned to ensure. This was emphasized to me in a conversation with the producer of one such show. Describing the role of the call takers to whom callers get through before reaching the host, the producer explained that one thing these operatives are required to do is to check that the caller is capable of making an argument, rather than simply reading from a written text. This seems designed to highlight the liveness and spontaneity of talk radio interaction.

sertions made by callers, but without necessarily taking on board issues of actual truth and falsity in those claims. Rather, the device is used to turn those claims against the caller him or herself.

The device in question takes the form of a "contrast structure" (Atkinson, 1984a; Drew, 1990; Mulkay, 1986; Pomerantz, 1988–1989; Smith, 1978) in which, first, a claim or version of events is attributed to the other, often (but not always) in the form of a direct quotation; and secondly, a problem with that version of events is identified, which in some way proposes or implies that the other's version is clearly at fault. The device takes the following general linguistic form:

You say (X), but what about (Y)?

where (X) and (Y) represent, respectively, the attributed claim and the competing version through which the fault in that claim is identified.

Using this device as the focal point of analysis, I will explore aspects of how hosts on talk radio use this procedure to pursue controversy in callers' contributions to the show. By the "pursuit of controversy" I mean the practice by which hosts routinely attend to callers' talk as potentially arguable and seek to define callers' claims and assertions as arguable actions, and so to locate, in the details of their talk, resources for building opposition.

ATTRIBUTING A POSITION AS A STRATEGY FOR ARGUING

There are numerous ways in which what someone said (or can be described as having said) is treated as the basis for a complaint, an accusation, or the taking of a skeptical stance, by being contrasted with what the *speaker* says or knows to be the case. For instance, M. H. Goodwin (1990) analyzes a "he-said-she-said" device for building a disputatious complaint in the talk of peer groups of African American preadolescent girls. This is a complex triadic format, in which one speaker, A, accuses another, B, of saying something about A to a third party, C, while A was not present, that something having subsequently been reported to A by C:

(1) Goodwin, 1990

1	Annette:	And Arthur said that you said that I was showin'
2		off just because I had that bl:ouse on.

Here, Annette accuses her addressee (Benita) of saying to Arthur that she, Annette, was "showin' off just because I had that bl:ouse on." Her evidence for this is that "Arthur said" that Benita had made such a comment. Although Goodwin does not focus on any contrastive dimension in this device, implicit in Annette's accusation here is her belief that she in fact was *not* "showin' off," which would contrast with the version of events reportedly stated by to Arthur by Benita.

A second way in which attributions can be involved in accomplishing skeptical talk is in the more straightforward third party accusations found in cases such as the following:

(2) NB:II:2:19

1 Nancy: A::nd ah, h he said that he: wss: had tried to
2 call 'er on Mother's Day an', h .hhhhhh a:n::d
3 he 'ad- (0.3) spent all da:y (.) yihknow tryin'
4 to call 'er: h [a:nd she:] (.) knows better than=
5 Emma: [°Mm hm:°]
6 Nancy: =tha:t because Roul never stayed home all day to
7 call anybod[y,h .hh
8 Emma: [n::No:,

Here, Nancy is both reporting and affiliating with the skepticism of her ex-husband's mother about a claim of the ex-husband (Roul) to have called his mother on Mother's Day. The turn is built in the form of a contrast between what Roul said (line 1 ff.) and what the mother "knows" (line 4: "she: knows better than tha:t"). Again, a triadic structure is invoked, between an absent accused (Roul), and two copresent parties, the reporter/complainant (Nancy) and the recipient of the complaint (Emma, who affiliates with Nancy's position in line 8). This is slightly different from extract (1), in which the triadic structure involves the complainant (Annette) and accused (Benita) being copresent, with the reporter (Arthur) absent.

A third variant, which is the one I will focus on in the present chapter, involves only two parties, complainant and accused, both of whom are copresent. In other words, in the "You say (X), but what about (Y)" device, the skeptical party does not use the reported speech of the other as the basis for a complaint, but uses their actual words (or a slight reformulation of them) as uttered just previously.

We can see how the device appears in arguments on talk radio with the help of extract (3). Here, the caller begins by putting forward a position on the issue of whether British laws forbidding general trading on Sundays should be repealed, so that shops could legitimately open for business 7 days a week. The host responds to this initially by clarifying a point of detail (lines 7–15). The device with which I am concerned is found in lines 16–21:

(3) H:30.11.88:2:1

1 Caller: I think we should (.) er reform the la:w on
2 Sundays here, (0.3) w- I think people should have
3 the choice if they want to do shopping on a Sunday,
4 (0.4) also, that (.) i-if shops want to open on a

5		Sunday th- th- they should be given the choice to
6		do so.
7	Host:	Well as I understand it thee: (.) the la:w (.)
8		a:s they're discussing it at the moment would allow
9		shops to open .h for six hou:rs, .hh [e:r] on a=
10	Caller:	[Yes.]
11	Host:	=Sunday,
12	Caller:	That's righ[t.
13	Host:	[From:, midda:y.
14	Caller:	Y[es,
15	Host:	[They wouldn't be allowed to open befo:re that.
16		.hh Erm and you talk about erm, (.) the rights of
17		people to: make a choice as to whether they
18		shop or not, [o:n] a Sunday,=what about .hh the=
19	Caller:	[Yes,]
20	Host:	=people who may not have a choice a:s to whether
21		they would work on a Sunday.

Focusing on lines 16–21, we find that the host first attributes a position to the caller (lines 16–18). The second thing is that he next puts forward a challenge that seeks to undermine the caller's view: "what about the people who may not have a choice a:s to whether they would work on a Sunday" (lines 18–21). The contrast structure with which the host constructs his challenge here involves juxtaposing an attributed position—"You say (X)"—with a competing version—"What about (Y)?"

The talk radio hosts in my data regularly use this "You say (X), but what about (Y)" device to exhibit skepticism of callers' accounts. The following extracts provide some further examples:

(4) H:26.1.89:2 ((Caller is female))

1	Caller:	.hh E:rm, uw- u-women've been fighting for
2		equalitie:s (.) e::r fo::r, u-yihknow many yea:rs,
3		.hhh an:d i-it seems to me that erm, they- want
4		their cake and eat it.
5		(0.5)
6	Caller:	Er:m,
7		(0.3)
8→	Host:	m-d- You s- You say you sa:y "the:y" but I mean:
9→		.hh er your voice seems to give awa:y thee erm,
10		.p fact that you're a woman too.

(5) H:21.11.88:16

1	Caller:	.hh people've been tr- saying the Russians've been
2		e:r, .hh ba::d an' the red- peril an' evrything for
3		(.) god knows 'ow many years an' now they're tryina
4		do something, .h everyone's saying the Queen

5 shouldn't go over=I don' understand the problem.
6→ Host: Well when you say ev'ryone it's actually:: thee,
7→ it's actually Downing Street the Prime Minister
8 who's saying that erm .h it is probably not a good
9 idea.

(6) G:3.2.89:8

1 Caller: I:t's a similar kinda thing to surrogate
2 mother:s. °.hh°
3 (0.2)
4 Host: Mmm?=
5 Caller: =Nob[ody m]i:nds- (.) surrogate mothers but they=
6 Host: [yes,]
7 Caller: =object to them being paid mone:y.
8 .h [I meh- i's- i's-]
9 Host: [Ho:w d'you mean a] n- er a- No: hang on a
10→ minute you're saying no:body mi:nds, duh su- err
11→ I think there's a lotta people who object to that.

(7) G:3.2.89:4

1 Caller: Ni::nety per cent of people, (.) disagreed with the
2 new propo:sals for thee N.H.S:. in the White Paper.
3 (0.8)
4 Host: You're- you're quite sure about that
5→ You say ni:nety per cent of the people disapprove
6→ uh- .h as if you have carried out your own market
7 rese:arch on this.

In each of these cases, as in extract (3), the host's turns take the form of contrast structures: In each case the first arrow indicates the attributed position, while the second points to the component that finds fault, and/or puts forward a competing version.

It is worth noting that the lexical structure of this "You say (X)" construction enables fault to be found in callers' talk in an especially argumentative or confrontational way. The three devices discussed so far in this section all involve "citatory" elements. That is, they all have speakers attributing positions to others by citing (some version of) their words. But these citatory elements operate in different ways according to the kind of interactional environment in which the talk is being produced. In the he-said-she-said device exemplified by extract (1), an absent party is being charged with responsibility for reporting a complainable action on the part of the accusee. Clearly, one upshot of this is that the accusee is thereby able to defy the accusation by denying that he or she ever said those things. In the more straightforward "he/she said" device exemplified in extract (2), it is the absent party him or herself who is being singled out as having made the claim, and thus as being responsible for whatever it is that is being complained about.

In the examples of "You say (X)" taken from talk radio disputes (i.e., extracts [3]–[7]), on the other hand, the citatory element of the device, and hence its accusatory properties also, are turned against the caller him or herself. This means that the device has an argumentative aspect actually built into it. We saw in chapter 2 that a basic feature of argument is the exchange of directly addressed positions and counterpositions. The "You say (X)" device is particularly effective in argumentative environments precisely because its first component directly allocates responsibility to a recipient for the claim that its second component shows to be at fault. The citatory properties of the device thus serve to locate fallibility not only in the substance of a claim, but in the person of the caller him or herself.

One of the things we can focus on in looking at these extracts is what exactly the host is finding fault with in the caller's talk, and how he is pointing up that fault. As stressed in chapter 2, opposition is a crucial feature of arguments. But insofar as "any utterance or action may contain objectionable features and [so] may become part of a dispute" (Maynard, 1985, p. 3), an important element of any analysis of the management of arguments (including those between hosts and callers) is the description of the local particulars of those utterances or actions that *do* get treated on actual occasions as arguables. By focusing on this aspect of the device, we can begin to see how hosts build opposition and pursue controversy by taking some element in the caller's talk and treating it as arguable through the contrastive "You say (X)" device.

As we will see throughout this chapter, the elements that are focused on tend to be relatively innocuous and uncontroversial words and phrases. For instance, in extract (3), it seems that the caller's use of the supposedly general category of "people," in his assertion that "people should have the choice if they want to do shopping on a Sunday" (lines 2–3), provides the host with a resource for building opposition. He subsequently treats that category as not general at all, and proposes that the caller's use of it in fact leaves out of account a quite different category of "people" (lines 20–21):

(1) Detail

16	Host:	... you talk about erm, (.) the rights of
17		people to: make a choice as to whether they
18		shop or <u>not</u>, [o:n] a Sunday,=what about .hh the=
19	Caller:	[Yes,]
20	Host:	=people who may n<u>o</u>t have a choice a:s to whether
21		they would <u>work</u> on a Sunday.

In a similar sense, recall that in extract (5), the host displayed a critical response to the caller's use of "people" as a general category. There, the caller began by describing the attitude of people toward "the Russians": People have been critical of the Russians in the past, but "now they're tryina do something, everyone's saying the Queen shouldn't go over" (lines 1–4). The host then dismantles that category and proposes that rather than being attributable to the general population, the view described by the caller actually is held by only one person: "the Prime Minister" (line 7).

Other types of generalization on the caller's part seem vulnerable to "You say (X)"-type critical rejoinders from hosts. In extracts (6) and (7), the remarks that are treated as arguables are assertions of a general and unmitigated character, such as "Nobody mi:nds surrogate mothers" (extract [6], line 5) and "Ni::nety per cent of people disagreed" (extract [7], line 1). In both these cases too, it is the unmitigated character of the callers' assertions that renders them arguable in the host's eyes.

The special significance of this can be drawn out in the following way. Unmitigated or "extreme case" formulations (like "*all* day," *totally* wrong," or "didn't say *anything*") are routinely used by speakers to support their positions, particularly where it may be felt that there is a special likelihood of doubt from a recipient (Pomerantz, 1986). Extreme case formulations can function to provide a sense of authoritativeness for a claim. In this sense, we see that in extracts (5) and (6), callers are using conventional resources for supporting a position and justifying a complaint. But in each case, hosts find fault precisely by treating these same features as the bases for arguing with the positions they are designed to justify. So that while extreme case formulations and related generalizations may be used to lend authority to versions in certain interactional environments, in others, particularly in argumentative environments, those kinds of statement may be exploited by a skeptical party to undermine the very positions speakers are using them to support.

The upshot of this is that hosts are provided with a formal resource that is particularly effective for building opposition within the interactional constraints of talk radio. Those constraints include the fact that in each individual call, the host, whose role is to respond to what the caller is saying, must, as it were, hit the ground running. Before the caller comes on the air, the host has little idea of the themes he or she will address, and even less idea of any particular statements he or she will make. The host may have access to a précis of the caller's proposed argument which is produced during the call-screening process. But this brief summary will not go into detail, and the caller is not bound to the version he or she initially provided once live talk starts on the air. Within this environment, the "You say (X)" device enables hosts to identify controversy by using apparently innocuous details of callers' talk as the basis for initiating or sustaining an argument. Put another way, use of the device means that hosts do not need to have much of an idea of what callers are getting at, nor do callers need to say anything especially controversial, to engage in argument on talk radio.

TURNING A CLAIM AGAINST ITSELF

I began this chapter by noting that "You say (X)" is a device used by hosts to undermine callers' arguments without necessarily dealing with their actual truth or falsity. This possibility is related to a general feature of contrast structures as skeptical devices. As both Pomerantz (1988–1989) and Drew (1990) have noted, the significant point about contrasts in disputatious talk is not whether or not the two versions are respectively true or false, but rather that the juxtaposition itself has the effect of encouraging a recipient or audience to *judge* that one of the versions is wrong. Drew (1992) shows how attorneys in cross-examination exploit this property of contrasts to project doubt about witnesses' evidence by simply leaving hanging a contrastive presentation of two apparently contrary details of a testimony: that is, not explicitly drawing any conclusion but leaving a silence in which the jury may draw the implicit conclusion for themselves. In a similar way, talk radio hosts can exploit the same properties to project doubt about the general validity of a caller's position by demonstrating faultiness in its details.

A number of extracts illustrate how hosts use the "You say (X)" device to construct a caller's opinion as arguable by emphasizing entirely innocuous details. The citatory element turns out to be very important here, because it allows hosts as skeptical parties to use the lexical structure of a claim itself as a resource for projecting doubt. This in turn means that hosts are able to cast aspersions without dealing with the issue of the claim's actual veracity or accuracy. This happens, for instance, in extract (7):

(7) G:3.2.89:4

```
Caller:   Ni::nety per cent of people, (.) disagreed with the
          new propo:sals for thee N.H.S:. in the White Paper.
          (0.8)
Host:     You're- you're quite sure about that
          You say ni:nety per cent of the people disapprove
          uh- .h as if you have carried out your own market
          rese:arch on this.
```

The host's ironic opposition here, in lines 5–7, does not work by opposing the caller's purportedly factual claim with a similarly factual claim (e.g., "You say ninety per cent of people disagree, but if you look at the real figures you'll see it's only sixty per cent"). Rather, the host uses his citation of the caller's claim to effectively turn it against itself by way of the common sense inference that ordinary citizens do not do market research in order to test public opinion. The format of the "You say (X)" device thus enables the host to pick on the caller's chosen way of putting her claim to propose that the claim must be at fault.

In extract (3) also, the device is used as a framework in which the caller's claim is turned against itself by means of the lexical choices made in formulating the argument. (Recall that the caller has just said "I think people should have the choice if they want to do shopping on a Sunday.")

(1) Detail

16 Host: . . . you talk about erm, (.) the rights of
17 people to: make a choice as to whether they
18 shop or not, [o:n] a Sunday,=what about .hh the=
19 Caller: [Yes,]
20 Host: =people who may not have a choice a:s to whether
21 they would work on a Sunday.

I have already remarked that the host here brings into play a collection of "people" left out of account in the caller's original use of that category. What is especially striking now, though, is the way in which the lexical format of the caller's statement that "people should have the choice" is mirrored in the host's turn: "what about the people who may not have a choice. . . ." This relates to a point made about the effectiveness of symmetry in contrastive devices by Atkinson (1984b), in his work on rhetoric in public speech-making. In speeches, contrasts occur regularly as strategies to elicit the audience's applause (see also Heritage & Greatbatch, 1986). Atkinson (1984b) shows that "for a contrast to work effectively in eliciting an immediate or early audience response, the second part should closely resemble the first in the details of its construction and duration" (p. 395). In extract (3), these two conditions are elegantly met. The symmetry between the sets of lexical items in which the critical contrast between "shop on a Sunday" and "work on a Sunday" is framed allows that contrast maximum hearability, both for the caller and for the overhearing audience.

Another potential of the citatory properties of the "You say (X)" device is illustrated in extract (8), where caller and host are arguing about a recent march by the National Union of Students, which ended in a confrontation with the police. The caller's position is in favor of the marchers over the police:

(8) G:26.11.88:3:1

1 Caller: Uh, what was supposed to happen yesterda:y, it
2 was an org- it was an o:rganized lobby of
3 Parliament by: the National Union of Students.
4 Host: °M:mm,°
5 Caller: And the idea was to make, .hh the public of
6 England, an' Great Britain, .h awa:re, .h of thee
7 loans proposals.
((...))
8 Host: You say it was an organized demonstration by the
9 National Union of Students.=[do y-
10 Caller: [No it was an or- it
11 was an organized lobby, .hh a:nd a ma:rch, which
12 was supposed to go [to ( )
13 Host: [Well you- you can organize a

lobby or a march it still amounts to a
demonstration=d'you think it got out of hand?

Here, we find the host picking up on a tiny detail of the caller's account—his use of the word "organized" (line 2)—and making argumentative capital out of that. The host uses the "You say (X)" format to build a contrast between the caller's description of the march as "organized" and an alternative version, "out of hand." The contrast is interrupted as the caller, himself focusing on the difference between the terms "lobby" (in his first version, line 2) and the host's more militant-sounding "demonstration" (line 8), interjects to correct the host's attribution.[2] But the host brushes aside this complaint and the contrast is eventually completed successfully. The host can assume that the overhearing audience, like he and the caller, know that the event in question did in fact end up in pitched battles between students and police, because this eventuality and its treatment in that morning's popular press have been the subject of previous calls. By means of citing the caller's description of the event as "organized," and then offering an alternative version in the form of a question to the caller: "d'you think it got out of hand?" (line 15), the host not only disagrees with the caller's version of events, but also casts doubt on the caller's competence as an observer of those events, and hence on his ability to take a reasoned position on the issue.[3]

In sum, use of the "You say (X)" device can show how closely hosts are monitoring callers' talk for potential arguables. The oppositions that are constructed frequently focus on very minor details of the caller's talk: use of extreme case formulations, generic references, or inappropriate descriptors. Moreover, the contrastive device not only works in the construction of controversy by locating empirical inconsistencies in a caller's account. Quoting a caller's assertion back and subsequently allowing it, through the contrast, to be *judged* as faulty enables hosts to project doubt about the verisimilitude of the caller's account without taking on the question of its actual truth or falsity.

RECOGNITION AND RESISTANCE

So far I have said nothing about how callers, as recipients of the kinds of skeptical moves analyzed in the preceding sections, respond to these moves and

[2]I return to consider some important features of this interjection by the caller in the next section.

[3]It is important to remember that callers themselves can always find ways of arguing back against these ironic contrasts. In the case in question, the caller does that later in the call by developing the position that a "breakaway group" belonging to a militant political faction caused the march to get "out of hand." He thus both preserves his own position as a supporter of the "organized" group and argues against the host's implications of incompetence.

to the interactional work that I have suggested they accomplish. I want to remark now on some of the ways in which callers (as well as hosts) orient to the "You say (X)" format as an effective device for exhibiting skepticism.

One way in which this can be observed is in callers' recognition that "You say (X), but what about (Y)" is a compound construction in which, the first part having been produced, speaker transition is not yet relevant, until the second part has appeared. This recognition is exhibited principally through callers' use of the standard conversational objects that Schegloff (1982) labels "continuers." Continuers are tokens such as "mm hm," or "uh huh," which display a recipient's understanding that a turn-in-progress is not complete, even though a possible transition-relevant place may have been reached. C. Goodwin (1986) shows that continuers are frequently placed at a particular point in the course of an ongoing turn, namely, at or near the end of one phrasal or sentential unit and extending into the beginning of another. In this way, continuers "bridge" turn-constructional units, and show their producers passing on what is a possible opportunity to take the floor. Looking back at extract (2), for instance, notice that Emma produces a continuer, "Mm hm," (line 5) at a point in Nancy's turn that bridges the end of one unit, "spent all da:y yihknow tryin' to call," and the beginning of the next, "a:nd she: knows better than tha:t . . .":

(2) NB:II:2:19

1 Nancy: A::nd ah, h he said that he: wss: had tried to
2 call 'er on Mother's Day an', h .hhhhhh a:n::d
3 he 'ad- (0.3) spent all da:y (.) yihknow tryin'
4 to call 'er: h [a:nd she:] (.) knows better than=
5 Emma: [°Mm hm:°]
6 Nancy: =tha:t because Roul never stayed home all day to
7 call anybod[y,h .hh
8 Emma: [n::No:,

It turns out, however, that Emma's "Mm hm," apart from bridging two phrasal units of Nancy's turn, also bridges two units of a different type: the two parts of a contrast structure beginning with "He said (X)." And without necessarily wanting to claim that Emma thereby specifically displays an orientation to the contrastive properties of Nancy's complaint, we can observe a markedly similar placement of continuers in the following excerpts from talk radio disputes:

(1) Detail

16 Host: . . . you talk about erm, (.) the rights of
17 people to: make a choice as to whether they
18 shop or not, [o:n] a Sunday,=what about .hh the=
19→ Caller: [Yes,]

Host: =people who may not have a choice a:s to whether
they would work on a Sunday.

In this fragment, "Yes" is used as a continuer (see Schegloff, 1982, p. 80). It comes, again, at what is hearable as the bridge between two units (i.e., "whether they shop or not" [line 18] is a possible phrasal ending, even though the host subsequently tags "o:n a Sunday" onto it). And again, the two units that the continuer bridges are, at the same time, the two parts of a contrast structure.

(9) H:21.11.88:11:3

Host: You sa:y that you would not force people to do it.
.h You do however accept that there is prejudice
against .hh er certain kinds of, homes and
er, [.hh] hospitals in communities [.hh] so .h=
Caller: [Yeh] [Yeh]
Host: =if: that prejudice exists people aren't going to
gi:ve ti:me. Or money for that matter.

In this extract, the caller's first continuer (line 5) comes rather later than in previous examples: It is placed *after* the host has projected the continuation of the turn with "and er . . ." But the second once more occurs precisely at the bridge between units: both phrasal units and contrast parts. Both continuers, like the "Yes" in extract (1), signal the caller's acceptance of the host's attributed version of their position. But what they also exhibit is the caller's recognition that, having produced this attribution, the host has not yet completed his turn, and is going on to produce a further component.

These excerpts, then, show that a "You say (X)"-type component, although not perhaps projecting a specifically contrastive "but . . . what about (Y)," nonetheless recognizably projects something more for the recipient. Callers can exhibit a recognition that hosts are using this utterance-type to do something more than simply quoting their assertions back at them.

More significant examples can be found, in which callers appear to be orienting in a stronger way to the particular *activity* for which hosts use "You say (X)": namely, the argumentative projection of doubt. We can observe this in cases where callers attempt to resist the skeptical potential involved in an attribution. In extract (10), host and caller are arguing about the problems caused by dogs fouling public walkways:

(10) H:2.2.89:12:1–2

Caller: U:sually when a dog fouls:, .hh e::r it, it
lea:ves-=the scent that is left behind even if
you:, clean up with boiling water an' disinfectant,
.hhh is a marker. .h An' when 'e comes on 'is

5		e::r, w:-wa:lk the next da:y, when 'e gets to that
6		ma:rk, he does the same thing again.
((...))		
7	Host:	er you s-seem to be suggesting that they go to
8		the same place every ti:me. Because they've been
9		there before.
10	Caller:	Ooh yes,=quite often ye:s.=
11	Host:	=Yeah but er(h)n(h) then:, .h e:r=
12	Caller:	=An[d other dogs will °also°.]
13	Host:	[this- this mea:ns that] they never go in a
14		different pla:ce,=doesn't it.

The host attributes to the caller the claim that dogs "go" in "the same place every ti:me" (line 8). In the second part of his contrast he casts doubt on this position by pointing out that "this mea:ns that they never go in a different pla:ce" (lines 13–14). Thus, the host uses the (attributed) extreme case formulation "same place every ti:me" to turn the caller's version against itself by implying that common sense tells us this could not be so.

Notice, however, that the host is actually *reformulating* the caller's claim. The caller began in a qualified manner by using the word "usually" (line 1), and his argument remains qualified in the sense that what he is saying amounts to something like "if the dog passes his own mark on another walk, he'll do the same thing again." This is somewhat different from the host's version: "they go to the same place every ti:me." It is noticeable then that the caller, in line 10, tags onto his apparently acquiescent "Ooh yes," the modifier "quite often." Thus, the caller, although appearing to be affirming the host's attribution, in fact is sustaining the more cautious version of his position. Clearly, if the caller's more cautious version were to be allowed to stand as a modification of the host's version, then the host could no longer complete the skeptical contrast he has begun. That is, "quite often" could not be effectively contrasted by the host's "never go in a different pla:ce."

The host deals with this by utterly ignoring the "quite often" component, and treating the prior turn simply as an affirmation. In line 11, the host displays his intention to go on to do the second part of the contrast he has set up. The caller, however, having heard the initial "Yeah but," interpolates a yet further modifier: "and other dogs will also" (line 12). But this time the host simply overrides his opponent, pressing on to complete the second contrast part in overlap with the caller's talk.

Similar features can be observed if we return to extract (8):

(8) G:26.11.88:3:1

1	Caller:	Uh, what was supposed to happen yesterda:y, it
2		was an org- it was an o:rganized lobby of
3		Parliament by: the National Union of Students.

4	Host:	°M:mm,°
5	Caller:	And the idea was to make, .hh the public of
6		England, an' Great Britain, .h awa:re, .h of thee
7		loans proposals.
((...))		
8	Host:	You say it was an organized demonstration by the
9		National Union of Students.=[do y-
10	Caller:	[No it was an or- it
11		was an organized lobby, .hh a:nd a ma:rch, which
12		was supposed to go [to ( )
13	Host:	[Well you- you can organize a
14		lobby or a march it still amounts to a
15		demonstration=d'you think it got out of hand?

Again, the host attributes to the caller a reformulated version of what was originally said. In this case, as I remarked earlier, the descriptor "organized lobby" is transformed into the more confrontational "organized demonstration" (line 8). The caller detects this substitution and seeks to combat it in lines 10–12, reasserting his own milder version and adding further modulating components (that the lobby was accompanied by a march, which was supposed to conduct people to a particular location; hence the lobby is shown to be the central activity, and the march was stopped by outside forces from reaching its destination).

But the host in this excerpt displays as clearly as the host in fragment (10) his intention to go on and complete the contrast in spite of the caller's interjection (lines 13–15). Rather than simply ignoring or overriding the interpolation, however, he begins by incorporating the caller's more cautious version within his own: "You can organize a lobby or a march it still amounts to a demonstration." He then rapidly goes on to produce the second contrast part with an utterance which, we can now observe, he had earlier begun (in line 9) in overlap with the caller's interjection: "d'you think it got out of hand?"

We thus find evidence of how callers both recognize and resist the contrastive and the skeptical nature of the "You say (X)" device. First, the use of continuers at the boundaries of "You say (X)"-type components demonstrates callers' recognition that such units can and indeed should project some further talk from the host. Secondly, callers' occasional attempts to modify hosts' attributions suggests that they also may recognize the potentially damaging skepticism achieved through this device, and can be seeking to resist such doubt-casting by hosts.

A final significance of this discussion is that it once again shows hosts pursuing controversy, and pursuing it singlemindedly with the use of a particular formal device. The attempt to build opposition is not derailed, in either of extracts (8) and (10), by callers' attempts to put forward more cautious claims than those attributed to them. Rather, hosts pursue the contrasts they have set up and succeed in casting the attendant aspersions regardless of callers' attempts at resistance.

CONCLUSION

This chapter has been devoted to the analysis of some interactional properties of one device for exhibiting skepticism and building opposition in arguments. I have focused on the use of the device in the talk radio setting, where it occurs with some regularity. However, a basic contention of conversation analysis is that many if not most of the verbal resources used by participants in institutional interaction have their home in ordinary conversation. This is because the organizational mechanisms of conversation are seen as general, and the specialized features that can be detected in institutional interaction are treated as systematic transformations of the basic conversational model (Sacks et al., 1974). As Zimmerman and Boden (1991) have put it: "To the extent that conversational organization is general, forms of talk unique to institutional settings should be rare. Instead, we should expect to find mundane forms selected and shaped to address the interactional contingencies of a given setting" (p. 12).

As I suggested at the beginning of the chapter, the "You say (X)" device is a generic argumentative device, which is related to other conversational devices through which speakers use what another said, or is accused of having said, as the basis for a display of skepticism or a disagreement. And although it is regularly found in the skeptical talk of hosts on talk radio, the device can also be found in related forms in many other settings, including everyday conversation.[4]

---

[4]Since beginning work on analyzing this phenomenon, I have located a number of examples drawn from settings other than the talk radio materials with which I began. Two examples follow. The first is taken from a television drama (and hence, interestingly, is a scripted instance of the device). The second comes from a broadcast news interview. Note especially here the same "recognition/resistance" features on the part of the interviewee as I described for callers' talk earlier in the chapter (lines 9–10):

(A) BBC TV:2.1.92 (Notebook)

1 Stark: You say your wife is neglecting her domestic
2 duties, neglecting the home. But Charlotte is
3 neglecting her<u>self</u> as well.

(B) WAO:21.8.84 [IE=Interviewee, IR=Interviewer]

1 IE: The death of Sean (Giles) was tra:<u>gi</u>c. I've
2 expressed my sympathy to his <u>fa</u>:mily.=But it is
3 the <u>Bri</u>tish who decided to use <u>vi</u>olence (.) to
4 use m<u>u</u>rder (.) to use <u>t</u>errorism. .h <u>I</u> could not
5 have foreseen that,

((...))

One thing we need to account for, though, is why, in my data at least, it is only hosts who use the "You say (X)" device. A significant feature of this chapter is that although I have shown how callers recognize the device and even orient to its use as a format for skepticism, no examples of callers actually using that format have been presented.[5] I want to suggest two related kinds of account for this asymmetry.

First of all, the fact that callers may orient to the first part of the device as recognizably projecting the contrary second suggests that the basic use of the utterance "You say (X) . . ." is as a preface to a dubitative counter. This core usage may itself account for the fact that callers appear not to use the device at all (at least, no cases crop up in all the calls I recorded and transcribed), whereas hosts use it with some regularity. A fundamental feature of interaction on talk radio is that callers are oriented to the task of presenting their opinion and, if necessary, defending it against the host's attacks. Therefore

---

6 IR: You say you have sympathy for the widow and
7 the child of Sean Downes
8 h[hh What do you:]
9 IE: [I have sympathy for every]body=
10 =[who has died in the past fifteen years.]
11 IR: [What (did you) have: for the]widows
12 and the children of RUC
13 me[n and British Army soldiers.
14 IE: [hh I have sympathy for everybody who has
15 died in the past fifteen years.

[5]Casual observation of TV and radio news interviews suggests that, while indeed interviewers use the "You say (X)" device pretty frequently, interviewees themselves deploy the device with more frequency than do callers in the talk radio data (though nowhere near as frequently as interviewers). Following is one example:

LRC:20.10.80

1 IR: Let's talk about the right to buy in terms of money
2 thou:gh, er some tenants not a great deal but some
3 have found that the: .hhh offers of discounts are very
4 attractive but when they get into the owning market as
5 they do (.) they find that repairs are not discounted
6 and that they're something they really can't handle.
7 This is a growing problem isn't it.
8→ IE: .hhh Well it u- it- it- I mean you talk about this as a
9 growing problem I think it's something like .hhh you
10 know between fi:ve and ten a week er- e:r are being
11 aske:d to: .hh for the councils to buy their houses
12 back. .hh I don't think that matters,

An obvious account for this is that in news interviews, particularly political interviews that take up much of the broadcast time of many news programs, interviewees are professional public figures who are well schooled in the cut and thrust of public speaking and debate. The same cannot be said of the ordinary citizens who make up the vast majority of callers to talk radio shows.

they will not be principally attuned to the host's remarks in a skeptical mode. Hosts, on the other hand, may typically be oriented to the task of pursuing controversy, finding something to argue with in what a caller is saying. In this sense, hosts adopt a stance of "professional skepticism" as regards callers' claims, hearing anything the caller says in terms of its potential arguability. The combination of these institutionally relevant task-orientations with the core usage of the "You say (X)" format suggests an explanation for the marked asymmetry in the use of the device between hosts and callers.

More than that, however, there is an important sense in which this device also works as a way for hosts to protect their occupancy of second position in disputes with callers. In chapter 3, I observed that the host initially occupies second position in arguments with callers by virtue of the sequential organization of calls. Callers, on the other hand, have to struggle to adopt second position by attempting to take on the role of challenger. Because it is the task of the caller, and not the host, to set the agenda for the call by expressing an opinion on some issue, taking on the role of challenger will be problematic for the caller unless the host explicitly expresses his own opinion. By using the "You say (X)" device, the host is able to exhibit skepticism of the caller's claim but still leave the caller in first position by requiring him or her to account for the fault that the device identifies.

Once again, then, the key feature of arguments on talk radio seems to be the distinction between first and second positions. In the previous chapter, I identified a number of second position argumentative resources by which the host may challenge the agenda-relevance of callers' remarks in an environment where the agenda is ostensibly set by the caller him or herself. "You say (X)" also appears to be a second position resource; however, it is significantly different from the agenda-contesting resources discussed in chapter 3. Through the use of "You say (X)," the host can challenge the caller's claims, but the second half of the device goes beyond requiring callers to account for their positions in their own terms, and sets up a possible alternative account, in terms of which callers are required to cast their account. In short, "You say (X)" is a second position device whereby the host can begin to construct a counterposition while still constraining the caller to defend his or her own position.

In the next chapter, some further techniques will be discussed whereby hosts and callers wrangle over the offensive in disputes; we turn to look at how interruptions are used as argumentative resources and how they may operate in the struggle to maintain or curtail participation in disputes.

5 The Uses of Interruption

A striking feature of talk radio discourse that has been at the heart of this book is its confrontational character. One way in which this confrontation talk is brought off is by the use of "interruption" as a verbal strategy to package classically argumentative actions such as challenges, rebuttals, and ripostes. The present chapter takes as its theme that use of interruption in argument sequences, and considers a number of aspects of how the activity of interrupting may be bound up with the accomplishment of confrontation talk on talk radio.

This sense of a relationship between interruption and confrontation has been explored before, notably by Schegloff (1988–1989) in his study of the notorious Bush–Rather encounter on U.S. TV; what was purportedly an interview given by then Presidential candidate George Bush to CBS anchorman Dan Rather turned into what was widely viewed as a confrontation between the two men. Schegloff remarks on how the confrontational trajectory of the encounter seems often to be marked precisely by the interruptive verbal behavior of the antagonists.[1]

In this chapter, I will pursue this theme in depth in relation to argument sequences on talk radio. The chapter begins from a particular standpoint: the idea that interruptions can be seen as having both a "sequential" and a

[1]A related point is made by Greatbatch (1992) in his study of the management of disagreements between antagonists in panel interview broadcasts: "[Interviewees] commonly *escalate* their disputes by (a) moving out of . . . their institutionalised footings, and (b) producing their talk interruptively" (p. 291, original emphasis).

"moral" dimension. The sequential dimension refers to the feature focused on in most research on the topic: the degree to which an interrupting turn is incursive with respect to ongoing speech. The moral dimension adds to that by focusing also on what interruption is being used to *do* in the local interactional context. Following, among others, Talbot (1992), I show how "attention to the occurrence of candidate interruptions [needs to] be coupled with attention to discoursal indications of interactants' perceptions of them *as* interruptions" (p. 451). This perspective will enable me to describe how interactants themselves appear to differentiate between "cooperative" and "confrontational" interruptions. Concentrating on confrontational interruption, I will discuss the ways in which hosts use interruption to exert strategic control over arguments with callers, as well as, once again, strategies of resistance on the part of callers.

INTERRUPTION, COOPERATION, AND CONFRONTATION

A major part of the reason why interruption is bound up with the escalation of confrontation in disputes is that interruptions are essentially incursive actions. As Talbot (1992) writes: "Interruptions are appropriations of a right to speak" (p. 458). Or, to adopt the technical argot of Sacks et al. (1974), to interrupt is to start a turn at talk in a place that is not a "transition-relevance place"; in other words, to start to speak while someone else is speaking and before that speaker's turn has reached a projectable completion point.

Interrupting also effectively denies, or at least challenges, the right of a current speaker to take his or her turn to such a completion point. Thus there is both a sequential and a moral dimension to interruption: Interruptions are violative on the level of turn-taking conventions and on the level of interpersonal relations.

Therefore, it would seem that interruption is by definition not only an incursive act, but also an intrusive, even hostile one. However, this is not quite the case. As Goldberg (1990) observes, speakers who produce utterances that on the purely sequential level interrupt another's speech may, on the interactional level, be doing either affiliative or disaffiliative actions. Goldberg distinguishes between interruptions that are "power" displays and those which display "rapport" by concentrating on what appear to be the motivations of their producers: "Given the multifunctional nature of interruptions, the analyst must be able to distinguish between those interruptions seemingly motivated by the interactional rights and obligations of the moment, and those seemingly produced to satisfy personal or interactional wants or needs" (p. 885).

Goldberg pays less attention to another dimension of this distinction, however, namely the different ways in which interruptees may react to being interrupted, thereby displaying their orientation to the affiliative or disaffiliative nature of the action. This distinction can be illustrated in the following way. One way that interruption may be responded to is by the current speaker rebuking the other for having made an illegitimate bid for the floor. Extract (1), taken from the talk radio data, is a particularly clear example:

(1) H:2.2.89:4:1-2

1	Caller:	As you can imagine I wuz absolutely::=livi[d(h)
2	Host:	[Well did
3		you- did you then ek- explain that- you-
4		un:derstood. that, yihknow do:gs have the call of
5		nature just as er as people do:[:,.hh] an' they=
6	Caller:	[eYe:s,]
7	Host:	=don't have the same kind of control, and so
8		the[refore th- s-so]
9	Caller:	[No::, but dogs] can be t[r a i : n e d,]
10	Host:	[m-I haven't fi]nished
11		so therefore thee owner, .hhh er whether you train
12		them or not is not really, quite the point, but the
13		owner, being there has the responsibility. . .

Here, the fact that the caller's bid for the floor in line 9 is treated by the host as an illegitimate incursion is clear from his reaction in line 10: "I haven't finished." Also noteworthy is the way in which he subsequently resumes the overlapped utterance at almost the exact point of interruption (line 11).

By contrast, in other cases where a speaker obviously starts up before a current speaker's utterance is finished, we do not find the incursion being subject to negative evaluation. Take the following instance, from ordinary conversation:

(2) NB:II:4:16

1	Nancy:	He's just a re:al sweet GU:y. .h .t [.hhhh
2	Emma:	[WONderful.
3	Nancy:	So: we were [sitting in]
4	Emma:	[YER LIFE] is CHANG[ing.
5	Nancy:	[EEYE::AH

Emma's turn in line 4 is interruptive in the sequential sense: It begins well before Nancy's line 3 turn has reached a projectable completion point. But to what extent might it be treated as interruptive on the *moral* dimension? Unlike the caller's turn in extract (1), which was produced and heard as a disaffiliative action (i.e., a disagreement), Emma's turn is an affiliative action in which she expresses her pleasure at the fact that Nancy (a divorcee) has found a new boyfriend (the "real sweet guy" Nancy refers to). Moreover, Nancy's recognition of the action's affiliative character is visible in the unhesitating and enthusiastic "EEYE::AH" with which she responds.

Thus, speakers who have been interrupted can respond in different ways to their coparticipants' action. They can react negatively or positively to an interruptive bid for the floor, depending on what kind of action they judge the interruptor to be engaging in. The actions we have looked at so far can be glossed as "cooperative" (affiliative/agreeing: extract 2) or "confrontational" (disaffiliative/disagreeing: extract 1).

This distinction is a key one for the analyses that will follow in the present chapter. Later, I will introduce some further features of the distinction as they relate to the case of confrontation talk on talk radio. But first it is worth pointing out that interruptors themselves can exhibit an orientation to these moral dimensions of interruption. This can be seen in the following case, also taken from the talk radio data, in which a host actually formulates what he is doing as "interrupting":

(3) G:26.11.88:7:1

```
Caller:   I'm actually phoning in: support of the stu:dents,
          .hh and also be[cause I::-
Host:                    [Wuh e-ca- can I just interrupt
          you, wu- [were] w-were you actually on the=
Caller:            [Yes.]
Host:     =demonstr[ation yesterday?
Caller:            [No:   I:   wasn't,
```

The host begins a question in a sequentially incursive position (line 3). But notice that he immediately interposes what amounts to an apology for this incursion: "can I just interrupt you." And the caller, a moment later, acknowledges the host's displayed orientation to his turn's interruptiveness, and assents to his taking the floor (line 5).

This case illustrates how, on occasion, the hostile or negative connotations that may attach to an interruptive bid for the floor can be prospectively neutralized by an interruptor. A speaker starting to talk in the midst of another's ongoing turn may use a component such as "Can I just interrupt you" in order to (a) exhibit an orientation to the possibility that this move may be negatively evaluated by the other, and (b) display that, in this case, no hostility is intended.[2]

[2] An opposite use of a speaker's formulation of some stretch of talk as an interruption is illustrated in Talbot (1992). The analysis centers upon an occasion in which a husband accuses his wife of interrupting him during his recounting, to friends, of an event from their recent holiday. In saying "I wish you'd stop interrupting me!" the husband transforms what appear to be his wife's attempts at collaborative involvement in telling the story, into "interruptions" of the husband's storytelling.

I now focus on the uses of interruption in hostile or confrontational talk in the course of disputes on talk radio. As I remarked at the beginning of this chapter, argumentative actions such as disagreeing, challenging, or rebutting may be packaged in the sequential form of an interruption. By focusing on what it is that the speaker is doing with that interruption in the local context of the talk, as well as on how the interruptee responds to being interrupted, we can gain further insights into how the sense of confrontation in talk radio disputes is interactively produced.

INTERRUPTION AND CONFRONTATION: PRESSING THE POINT HOME

In the following extended fragment of conflict talk from a talk radio call, the dispute between the caller and the host seems to become progressively more confrontational. A number of interruptions occur in the course of the excerpt (marked by arrows). This series of interruptions seems to mark the increasingly confrontational trajectory as each participant tries to press home his or her point.

The extract is taken from the "Princess of Wales" call, parts of which have been discussed in previous chapters. The caller has complained, among other things, about the price of tickets for a ball the Princess of Wales will attend. The host's response is that the money, so he believes, is going "to charity." This extract begins at the point where the caller, in response to this claim, has shifted the line back to an earlier complaint about the price of the Princess' hotel suite.

(4) H:2.2.89:3:2

1	Caller:	. . .but a thou:sand pounds a night at e- a
2		he- at a hotel is: (.) [I: think is still=
3	Host:	[Weh- n- n-
4	Caller:	=o[bscene.
5	Host:	[S:o you think it's all right the:n,
6		er::m if: they pay a thousand pounds to go
7		to this ba:ll, .h i[f it's for ch]arity.
8	Caller:	[No:::,]
9	Caller:	I:. well if- well I suppo:se so yes but I
10		mean if it go:es to charity but we're not
11		told that. (.) But I mean I [don't know (the)-
12→	Host:	[Well what d'you
13		think it's going to.
14	Caller:	I've no- 'aven't a clu::e,
15		(.)
16	Host:	E:r, well if you haven't a clu::e,

17		you m[ight-
18→	Caller:	[Ye:h well I mean whe:re d'you [think it's]
19	Host:	[you- you]=
20	Caller:	=[going] to.]
21	Host:	[might've]] I think it's going to charity.
22	Caller:	Yeh but you don't know do you.
23	Host:	Ehrm I'm almost su:re.
24		(.)
25	Caller:	We:ll,
26		(.)
27	Caller:	[[Al-
28	Host:	[[But you had no idea.
29	Caller:	No I- well I['m being honest.]
30→	Host:	[And you came to a] con-=
31	Caller:	=[You don't] know ei:[ther.
32	Host:	[You had- yi] [You came to a conclusion
33		wuthahdenny- without any idea and without even
34		taking it into consideration.
35	Caller:	But I still think all right, weh- we don't know
36		where the money's going to (whether) charity but
37		I still think a thou:sand pou:nds a night at a
38		hote:l, .hhh a:nd the fact that she's going on to
39		visit p- ho:meless people. . .

In this extract we see three instances of sequentially incursive utterances representing interactionally hostile actions (lines 12, 18, and 30). One way that these interruptions are used is as part of each speaker's attempt either to gain, or to keep hold of, the argumentative initiative.

Just before the extract begins, as I remarked, the caller has backed down in the face of the host's retort that the money for the ball is going to charity. Lines 5–11 show the host following up that small victory, and the caller conceding his point. A moment later, however, the caller appears to attempt another line of argumentative attack (line 11), using the disjunctive, "But I mean I// don't know the. . . ." It is in the midst of this utterance, at a point where (a) it is clear that the caller has embarked on a next turn component, but (b) nothing substantive has been said, that the host interrupts with a challenge (line 12). In the next section, I return to consider some significant features of this first interruption. For the moment, notice that with this move, the host succeeds in maintaining the argumentative initiative he had gained just prior to the excerpt's opening, effectively blocking the caller's attempt to raise some next matter, and as it turns out, starting up a to-and-fro, who-knows-what argument that takes up most of the rest of the excerpt.

It is in the course of this who-knows-what confrontation that the two further instances of confrontational interruption found in the fragment occur. I want to focus on the ways in which the participants' reactions to being interrupted play a significant role in framing this spate of talk as a "confrontation." In line 18, the caller, who so far has been on the defensive against the host's attacks on her complaint, suddenly takes up an aggressive stance, interrupting him with a challenge that mirrors his prior interruptive challenge to her (in lines 12–13). The host's reaction to this takes a particular form: That is, he refuses to cede the floor cleanly once the caller's interruption is under way. In other words, as she interrupts him, he responds by trying to carry on with the overlapped utterance.

The significance of this reaction can be brought out in the following way. At least in certain noncombative conversational environments, it is very frequently the case that speakers who are interrupted rapidly drop out of competition for the floor (Jefferson, 1986; Jefferson & Schegloff, 1975). For instance, in fragments (5), (6), and (7), which come from everyday conversations, the overlapped speakers readily cede the floor soon after the onset of overlap:

(5) SBL:2:2:3:38

1	Zoe:	an' he sorta scares me, h
2	Amy:	Have you seen 'im?
3	Zoe:	.hhh We:ll I(m) I've met 'im,
4→	Amy:	.hhhhh Well uh actually: [when she's-
5	Zoe:	[An' the way the:y pla:y.
6		Oh:-
7		(.)
8	Amy:	Serious huh?
9	Zoe:	.h Yah,

(6) TRIO:2:III:1

1	Marjorie:	We:ll? She doesn't kno:w. uhhh:
2		huhh [huh-huhh-huh-huh-heh-heh]
3	Loretta:	[O h h m h y G h o : d,]
4→	Marjorie:	hhhhh Well it [was an-
5	Loretta:	[Are you watching Daktari:?
6		(0.2)
7	Marjorie:	nNo:,
8		(.)
9	Loretta:	Oh my go:sh Officer Henry is (.) ul-locked in the
10		ca:ge wi- (0.3) with a lion.

(7) SBL:2:2:3:42-3

1	Claire:	So: uh::::: she said [don't worry about i:t=
2	Chloe:	[Mm hm,
3	Claire:	=an:d so an' I jus' thought .hh the nex' ti::me
4→		u-that [I have-
5	Chloe:	[No:w uh see Pat anno:ys my Frank. hh
6		(0.3)
7	Claire:	Ye:ah.

8 (0.2)
9 Chloe: Uh he:'s told me that.

Note the way in which the speakers who are overlapped, rather than attempting to finish their sentences, abandon what they are saying in midphrase (arrowed lines). This type of dropping out of competition for the floor is one routine way in which participants orient to the *minimization* of overlap in ordinary conversation (Jefferson & Schegloff, 1975; Sacks et al., 1974; some other techniques are discussed in Schegloff, 1987). At the same time, however, we can notice that in each case, the overlapping turn mentions something slightly disjunctive from what the current speaker seems about to say—yet in none of the cases does the overlapped speaker overtly sanction the other for engaging in a morally dubious activity. Indeed once speakers have dropped out, each one subsequently topicalizes the other's line with short utterances like "Serious huh?" or "No:," or "Ye:ah."[3]

By way of contrast, we can look at the talk radio host's reaction to being interrupted in extract (1). I noted earlier that one way the host displays his negative evaluation of the caller's overlap is by (a) announcing, as the caller is speaking, that he hasn't "finished," and subsequently (b) explicitly resuming his utterance at its cut-off point.

(1) H:2.2.89:4:1-2

1 Host: We:ll did you- did you then ek- explain that- you-
2 un:derstood that, yihknow do:gs have the call of
3 nature just as er as people do:[: .hh] an' they=
4 Caller: [eYe:s,]
5 Host: =don't have the same kind of contro:l and so
6 the[refore th- s- so]
7 Caller: [No::, but dogs] can be t[rai:ned,
8 Host: [m-I haven't
9 finished, so therefore thee owner,...being there
10 has the responsibility. . .

We can see that the host displays less of a concern to minimize overlap than the overlapped speakers in excerpts (5)–(7). To be sure, just after the caller starts up in line 7, the host cuts off in a similar way to those speakers: "so

[3] I have worded my claim carefully here: "in none of the cases does the overlapped speaker *overtly* sanction their coparticipant. . . ." For it can be noted that in each case the topicalizing particle ("Serious huh?", "Ye:ah" etc.) is preceded by a tiny pause. Given previous work showing the potential significance of such small gaps in, for instance, adumbrating disagreement or other unfavorable responses (Davidson, 1984), it may be possible that these little pauses comprise a fleeting but significant display of an overlapped speaker's negative evaluation of the overlap. However, the central points as far as the main argument is concerned (i.e., overlapped speaker's readiness to cede the floor, and subsequent production of a topicalizing particle) stand.

the//refore th-" (line 6). However, he immediately attempts to restart his overlapped phrase: "s- so," before cutting off again just prior to explicitly sanctioning the caller's interruption (lines 8–9).

In the following detail from our extended extract (4), we see a similar phenomenon. The host (a) cuts off just after overlap onset (line 17), but then (b) attempts, while the caller is still speaking, to restart the second part of his interrupted "if–then" construction (line 19):

(4) Detail

16	Host:	E:r, well if you haven't a clu::e,
17		you m[ight-
18→	Caller:	[Ye:h well I mean whe:re d'you [think it's]
19	Host:	[you- you]=
20	Caller:	=[going] to.[
21	Host:	[might've] [I think it's going to charity.
22	Caller:	Yeh but you don't know do you.
23	Host:	Ehrm I'm almost su:re.

Unlike in extract (1), where the host retrieves his own line following the caller's interruption, here the host's next full turn, in line 21, is a response to the caller's interruption. But his initial unwillingness to cede the floor to her interruption again illustrates the point that the confrontational or combative nature of an interruption can be highlighted precisely by the reactions of interrupted speakers themselves.[4]

Later in the excerpt we see a third spate of interruptive talk, during which both participants engage in a battle for the floor with the result that they appear to be talking over one another in a simultaneous attempt to press home their respective points:

(4) Detail

28	Host:	But you had no idea.
29	Caller:	No I- well I[’m being honest.]
30	Host:	[And you came to a] con-=
31	Caller:	=[You don't] know ei:[ther.
32	Host:	[You had- yi] [You came to a conclusion
33		wuthahdenny- without any idea and without even
34		taking it into consideration.

[4]The point I am making here goes directly against Beattie's (1983) argument about interrupted speakers holding and not holding the floor. In his account, if a speaker tries to hold the floor, it renders the attempted interruption "unsuccessful": A "successful" interruption sees the overlapped speaker losing the floor. This seems to be a case of the sequential/moral confusion I discussed earlier. On my account, it is significant that overlapped speakers try to hold the floor through the interruption, precisely because this is a way they can display their own orientation to the interruptiveness of the other's move.

Notice again the marked lack of overlap minimization, this time in the caller's utterances in lines 29 and 31. On both occasions, finding herself speaking in overlap with the host, she continues sentences to completion, rather than abandoning them and withholding talk until she is in the clear. Again, although the host does cut off utterances in midword (for instance, in line 30), notice his persistent attempts to recycle the same utterance, "You came to a conclusion . . ." (in lines 30, 32, and 32–34). Schegloff (1987) has observed that this kind of recycling or redoing of a turn beginning is one of a number of systematic ways of dealing with the situation of finding oneself speaking in overlap with another. In this case, the host uses such a technique in response to the caller's refusals to abandon her turns, while attempting to get in his argumentative move in the clear.

The upshot of all this is that in extract (4), we find a stretch of talk that is combative and confrontational not only in terms of subject matter, but also in terms of how it is handled. In the sequences I have discussed, talking interruptively, and indeed reacting to a coparticipant's talk as interruptive, are bound up with the interactional framing of a strip of confrontational talk.

"REINING BACK"

So far I have shown some ways in which interruption can be viewed as a communicative deed rather than as merely a type of speech overlap, and analyzed as a moral feature of interactional environments. I now focus on the use of one particular form of interruption as a strategy for doing confrontation in talk radio disputes. This is a strategy found most commonly in the talk of the host, and it involves interrupting to "rein back" the development of the caller's line of argument.

In the following detail from extract (4), we find the host interrupting the caller in a particular sequential location, which Jefferson (1986) has referred to as "post-continuation":

(4) Detail

9	Caller:	I:, well if- Well I s'po:se so yes but I
10		mean if it go:es to charity but we're not
11		told that. (.) .h But I mean I [don't know the-
12	Host:	[Well what d'you
13		think it's going to.
14	Caller:	I've no- 'aven't a clu:e.

At line 11, the caller comes to the recognizable completion of a sentence: "But we're not told that." After a slight pause, she holds the floor by starting on a next sentence: "But I mean . . ." However, before this new sentence has really gone anywhere, the host produces a retort to the previous point (lines 12–

13). In this case, to quote Jefferson's (1986) description, the host starts to speak "just after the [caller] has produced a clear indication of going on, following a possible completion" (p. 159).

Jefferson (1986) shows that this is a systematic place for overlapping talk to occur. And because the current speaker has given the indication that he or she wishes to carry on speaking following a possible completion, postcontinuation is a place where overlapping talk may become hearably and warrantably interruptive. Once again, however, the distinction between cooperative and confrontational uses of such a sequential form is significant. Jefferson (1986) focuses on postcontinuation interruptions that package affiliative responses to something that was just said, as in the following examples:

(8) SBL:3:1:6

```
1      Amy:       all that stuff Marylou? requires a lo::tta
2                 spa:ce. I me┌an ih .hhh
3→     Marylou:               └Specially if you're gonna have it
4                 open for the public,
```

(9) SCC:DCD:26

```
1      Bryant:    that brai:ding that wouldn't of been touched
2                 with an i:ron. The m┌o:st we'd've done┐
3→     Sokol:                         └O h : n o   a : l┘right,
4                 steam.
```

(10) NB:IV:4:4

```
1      Emma:      cuz you see she was: depending on: him takin'
2                 her in to the L.A deeple S:- depot Sundee
3                 so ┌'e says┐
5→     Nancy:        └  I:'ll ┘ take 'er in:
```

In each case here, the second speaker's move is in some way interruptive; but it is also affiliative. The arrowed turns are interruptive in that they begin one or two syllables into what is clearly a continuation on the current speaker's part, following the completion of a sentence or phrase. But those turns package affiliative actions. For instance, in (10), Nancy's turn in line 5 is an offer of help with the trouble encountered by Emma's daughter in getting to "the L.A. depot Sundee." And in (8) and (9), Marylou and Sokol, respectively, are producing varieties of agreement with their coparticipants (in the latter case, Sokol's "Oh: no a:lright, steam" evidently represents a backdown from a previous assertion).

What I want to focus on here, by contrast, is the use of postcontinuation interruptions to engage in argumentative or confrontational talk by hosts in the talk radio setting.[5] For instance, in line 12 of extract (4), the host uses

[5]Note that I am not arguing here that post-continuation interruptions are only used combatively on talk radio, nor that the form is only used affiliatively in everyday conversation. The dis-

postcontinuation interruption to respond to a remark of the caller's that he has identified as an arguable action, though from which the caller's line of talk may be about to move on. Following "we're not told that" in line 11, the caller leaves a micropause before taking a short breath and indicating a disjuncture: "But . . ." Clearly, one thing she could be doing here is moving on to some next point in her argument. But that possibility is blocked by the host as he jumps in with an interruption that effectively reins back the line to preserve the topicality of the prior point as an arguable claim.

Looking at some further examples of postcontinuation interruption in talk radio arguments, we find a recurrence of this reining back feature. In extracts (11), (12), and (13), the host interrupts a clear continuation on the caller's part to rein back the line of talk, having identified an arguable action which, by virtue of a possible move on to some next point, is in imminent danger of losing its relevance. However, a further striking feature emerges in these cases, which itself is related to the confrontational nature of this set of interruptions: In each case, the amount of talk that goes by following a syntactic/intonational completion point before the host's interruption is substantially more than was the case in extracts (8)–(10), earlier:

(11) H:21.11.88:11:1-2

```
   Caller:  the thing that worries me is that I think it
            actually creates a sense of separateness between
            the people who're giving and the people who
            get. [(0.8) If you try:] [to-
→  Host:         [     (1.2)       ] [Well there is a
            separateness without the telethon.
```

(12) H:21.11.88:11:1

```
   Caller:  I think this is a- a clea::n way of giv- of getti-
            get- salving your conscience, to just pick up
            the credit ca:rd and uh .hh .t .k pay the
            money. [.h There's a big contra] [diction-
→  Host:           [       (1.0)           ] [Well if people want
            to do that why not.
```

(13) G:26.11.88:7:1

```
   Caller:  My real point is that I'm: very concern:ed, .hh
            about thee, (0.5) kh the lack of freedom of
            speech in this country at the moment.
            [.hhh Erm, this first ca] [me to my:-
→  Host:    [      (1.4)            ] [What do you mean by-
            What d'you mean by that Ann,
```

---

tinction is between the uses of the same structural phenomenon in two different interactional activities (affiliating/arguing) and not between "talk radio" and "ordinary conversation" as interactional contexts per se.

In these extracts, callers continue in active speakership following a possible transition place for 1 to 1.5 seconds. In contrast to the one-and-a-bit syllables of the continuations in extracts (8)–(10), these continuations proceed for between three and five syllables before hosts' utterances begin.

Most graphic in this regard is extract (11). There, the caller completes a sentence in line 4 with "the people who get." This is followed by a substantial pause of 0.8 seconds. It is only after the caller has produced three complete words of his next sentence that the host comes in with a riposte, in line 5.

There are, then, two major ways in which the argumentative and confrontational uses of postcontinuation interruptions can be traced in these extracts. One way in which this second set differs from the first (extracts 8–10) is in terms of the sheer amount of talk that the host lets go by before making his bid for the floor. That kind of "deep incursion" lends these examples a greater sense of interruptiveness and contributes to the confrontational aspects of the dispute.

The other way is that, in each case, the host interrupts a continuation by the caller in order to rein back the line of talk, to respond to an arguable action which the continuation puts in possible danger of losing its local contextual relevance. That property of reining back allows hosts to preserve the topicality of arguable points about to be moved on from, and thereby to sustain the argumentative nature of their interactions with callers.

INTERRUPTION AND PARTICIPATION CONTROL

Interruptions are often thought to be involved with the establishment or maintenance of power in interaction, particularly in what are taken to be asymmetrical encounters such as those between lay and professional persons (Davis, 1988), or, on a more general level, between men and women (West & Zimmerman, 1977, 1983). As West and Zimmerman (1977) put it: "The use of interruptions is *in fact* a control device, since the incursion . . . disorganizes the local construction of a topic" (p. 527). A similar view underpins Davis' (1988) account of the use of interruptions to control topics in doctor–patient interactions: "Control over topicality is one of the primary ways that power is exercised by professionals in institutional encounterings" (p. 304).

In the case of talk radio, one way in which hosts can exert a form of institutional control in practical sequential terms is through their use of a particular strategy involving what Jefferson (1981) has called "post-response-initiation" interruption. Recalling the theme of chapter 3, this is a form of interruption bound up with hosts' role as second position challengers of callers' agendas. And in a similar way to some of the strategies discussed at the end of that chapter, hosts may use post-response-initiation interruption to constrain the participation options open to callers at certain moments.

For an example of this configuration we can look back again at extract (4), and recall that the third instance of interruption found there involved the host starting up a turn midway through the caller's response to an accusation:

(4) Detail

28	Host:	But you had no idea.
29	Caller:	No I- well I[’m being honest.]
30	Host:	[And you came to a] con=
31	Caller:	=[You don't] know ei:[ther.
32	Host:	[You had- yi] [You came to a conclusion
33		wuthahdenny- without any idea and without even
34		taking it into consideration.

In the first three lines we find the following three things occurring: (a) The host produces an accusation (line 28), (b) the caller embarks on a response to that accusation (line 29), and (c) the host interrupts that response with a turn pursuing the initial accusation (lines 30–34).

A similar configuration, structurally speaking, can be found in the following extract:

(14) H:21.11.88:11:3

1	Caller:	.h Well giving ti:me would actually bring the
2		people together.
3	Host:	Mbu- d-d- But you're suggesting they should be
4		ma:de, to do it?
5	Caller:	No: no, what I'm suggestin[g i:s,
6	Host:	[Well if the prejudice
7		exists they're not going to do it.
8	Caller:	Well what I- what I'm suggesting i- should be
9		do:ne. . .

In lines 3–4, the host produces a question-intoned turn, thereby soliciting a response from the caller. In line 5, the caller responds by first negating the host's claim about what he is suggesting, then going on to offer his own formulation of his argument ("what I'm suggesting i:s . . ."). But in line 6 the host interrupts this response with a turn which, in a similar sense to the previous excerpt, follows up his original question, as it were "bringing the point home."

Jefferson (1981) notes some similar uses of this kind of post-response-initiation interruption as a way of following up a prior statement or question. In particular, she observes that it seems to be used in dealing with "unfavorable" responses on the part of recipients. In this paper, Jefferson's central phenomenon is the "post-response pursuit of response": a device whereby speakers "attempt to elicit revision of a problematic response by proposing, in effect, that the response did not occur, and response is due" (p. i). Extract (17) is an example:

(15) Br.Pr.1.2.1 ((From Jefferson, 1981. Free translation of original German. Taken from a psychiatric interview.))

1	Dr. F:	I understand (0.8) ( ) that you're not
2		feeling very well.
3	Mary:	Yea::h well that is [the opinion]
4→	Dr. F:	[Is that correc]t?
5	Mary:	of Doctor Hollmann.
6	Dr. F:	Uh [huh
7	Mary:	[But it isn't mine.

This form of asking for a response after a response has been initiated is, Jefferson (1981) suggests, "an attempt to counter, override, interrupt, an unfavorable response-in-progress" (p. 13). The response is unfavorable because it is not the response the doctor was after: He can interpret Mary's "Yea::h well . . ." (line 3) as indicating an upcoming disagreement (Pomerantz, 1984a) with his description of her condition as "not feeling very well" (i.e., as in a condition possibly to be readmitted to the psychiatric hospital; see Bergmann, 1992).

In a similar way, hosts on talk radio may use this form of countering or overriding a response-in-progress to deal with unfavorable responses. This device can operate as a means of constraining the options open to callers in formulating a response to a question or challenge:

(16) BC:I:G:15 ((Taken from an American talk radio show.))

1	Host:	Haven't you bothered to check your facts on any
2		of this.
3	Caller:	Yes,
4	Host:	Well then you should know, that a Congressman, or
5		any member of the Congress of the United States,
6		is immune to arrest under certain types of charges,
7		during the time the Congress is sitting.
8	Caller:	Mm hm
9	Host:	Didn't you know that?
10	Caller:	But that's [( )
11→	Host:	[Didn't you know that?
12	Caller:	I unders- I know that.
13	Host:	If you knew that why did you ask me.

(17) H:21.11.88:6:1

1	Caller:	I: have got three appeals letters here this week.
2		(0.4) All askin' for dona:tions. (0.2) .hh Two from
3		those that I always contribute to anyway,
4	Host:	Yes?
5	Caller:	.hh But I expect to get a lot mo:re.
6	Host:	So?

7 Caller: .h Now the point is there is a limi[t to ( )
8→ Host: [What's that got
9 to do- What's that got to do with telethons
10 though.
11 Caller: hh Because telethons yesterda:y, (0.6) e::rm was
12 appealing to people, (.) to: send in for various
13 things...

In both these cases the host cuts into a response-in-progress in order to redo the question (in [16] it is a straight repeat, in [17] a recycled version) because he judges from what he has heard of the response so far that it is somehow unacceptable. In extract (17), the caller's "Now the point is . . ." (line 7) evidently does not address, for the host, the challenge implied in his previous turn. In his next turn (lines 8–9),[6] he elaborates or explicates that challenge. In the previous fragment, extract (16), the caller responds to "Didn't you know that?" by saying "But that's . . .", which may well imply an unspoken affirmative (i.e., "Yes, but that's . . ."). This is not acceptable for the host, however. He evidently wants the caller to actually say "Yes I know that," and interrupts to press for this acceptable response.

In these cases, hosts are successful in enforcing restrictions on the options available to callers for responding to a question or challenge. Notably, in both cases, callers substantially reshape their responses following the repeat question, in such a way as to address the question in the way the host seems to desire. For instance, in (16) the caller does indeed say "I know that" (line 12), which in turn allows the host a strategic follow-up with his next question: "If you knew that why did you ask me."

One way, then, in which talk radio hosts can use interruption as a control device is to cut into an unacceptable response-in-progress in order to press for a response that would be acceptable. Clearly, it is not open only to hosts to engage in this practice. There is no rule or process which disables callers from producing post-response-initiation interruptions in order to press for acceptable responses. Yet the fact is that in all the calls I have recorded and transcribed, I find no examples of callers doing this.

We can account for this phenomenon by once again invoking the argument about first and second positions which is at the center of my claims about the structure of disputes on talk radio. I have stressed the ways in which the distribution of turn-positions vis-à-vis an arguable claim can be loosely mapped

[6]This turn is not strictly an interruption because the caller's "Now the point is there is a limit" *could* be heard as a possibly complete utterance. We could say that it turns out to be interruptive because the caller does not in fact stop after the word "limit" but carries on, briefly, in overlap with the host. Nonetheless, the sense of interruptiveness, of the host cutting in to follow up his prior turn, remains clear on the actual tape recording (which unfortunately you are not able to hear), even if it appears less evident in the transcription.

onto an asymmetrical distribution of interactional prerogatives and argumentational devices. In the case of talk radio, one aspect of this asymmetrical distribution is that hosts and callers, respectively, are in offensive and defensive positions in relation to callers' opinions for much of the call. This leads to hosts issuing hostile questions and challenges to callers far more frequently than callers do to hosts. And this, in turn, makes for a greater likelihood that the post-response-initiation interruption strategy, which is based on asking a question and subsequently constraining the response options available to the answerer, will be adopted by hosts.

CONCLUSION

Throughout this chapter I have sought to treat interruption as a feature of the social construction of arguments. I have analyzed some of the ways in which interrupting and being interrupted are practical resources by which disputants can frame their talk as confrontational. I have also illustrated some of the ways in which, in the talk radio setting, interrupting can be used as one form of control strategy, mainly by hosts.

In much research on interruption, interrupting is seen as a conversational strategy that is linked to relations of power. For instance, in West and Zimmerman's work (1977, 1983), it is claimed that men interrupt women more frequently than the opposite, and this is linked to a more general claim that men occupy a position of power vis-à-vis women. This work itself has been the subject of a great deal of controversy (see, especially, Talbot, 1992). Most of the controversy, however, has centered around West and Zimmerman's claims about the relationship between gender relations and interruption patterns, and not around their claim that interruption is related to the local distributions of power in talk-in-interaction. For instance, although Talbot (1992) takes issue with the empirical and theoretical status of West and Zimmerman's claims about gender, she in fact argues for a much more interactionally sensitive analysis of the ways in which interruption may indeed be strategically used to establish a power relationship in some stretch of talk. In line with such a view, later sections of this chapter have considered how talk radio hosts are in a position to use interruption to exercise power within the interaction by constraining the participation options open to callers.

However, although we might want to say that the host therefore wields institutionalized power over the caller (in the same way that West and Zimmerman, 1983, suggest men wield power over women by interrupting them more frequently and in different ways), such an account must not act only as a gloss on the ways that power is actually instantiated, and thus reproduced, on specific interactional occasions. In order to adequately analyze power in discourse we need to observe *how* it is instantiated through particular interactional strategies, and to consider the interplay between interaction processes themselves and the organizational features of the setting. This chapter has touched on that issue by tying together certain interruptive strategies and the asymmetries between first and second positions in talk radio disputes. The next chapter addresses the same issue by examining an aspect of those disputes that is very significant from the point of view of power and the insitutional nature of talk radio: that is, the endings of arguments.

6 Endings and Outcomes

This chapter is concerned with how arguments are terminated on talk radio. The fact that hosts are always in a position to cut off callers whose opinions they find disagreeable is often noted as a significant index of the power relations in play on talk radio (Moss & Higgins, 1984; Verwey, 1990). But although that feature has been noted, the precise ways in which the termination of calls is managed has not been analyzed. In this chapter I provide such an analysis, and in the process show how this can bring another dimension to my key theme of how asymmetry and power on talk radio are connected to the distinctions between first and second positions in arguments.

As I suggested in chapter 3, one upshot of the organization of calls is that hosts, unlike callers, are able to select the point within the call at which they will set out their own view on the issue in question. In my data, one place where hosts routinely do this is at the *end* of the call. This is a juncture that provides hosts with an argumentative opportunity that is not open to callers. At this point, the host is able to close down the caller's channel of verbal access to the dispute, and so put an argument forward without allowing his opponent any chance to respond. While the caller may of course choose to "hang up" on the host, and so unilaterally close the argument, he or she can only do this by withdrawing from the interactional arena, and thereby withdrawing from the argument. In the final stages of the call, therefore, the host may adopt first position without allowing the caller any challenging prerogative. The host's initial power to challenge the caller while refraining from putting a view of his own thus becomes, at the end of the call, the host's power to put his own point of view without allowing the caller to respond with any counter-position.

In this chapter I will provide a detailed examination of how that power is instantiated in talk. In the process, some important features of the distinctive public nature of interaction on talk radio will come to the fore. By concentrating on the final stages of arguments between hosts and callers, I will locate another dimension to the relationship between distinctive institutional asymmetries and power in interaction. As we will see, the ways in which the endings of calls are accomplished, and their outcomes determined, lends a greater significance to the technical features of the mediated nature of talk radio disputes (i.e., the fact that they take place via the telephone and, most importantly, on the radio).

TERMINATING CONFLICT EPISODES

I begin by outlining the techniques by which arguments are terminated. In general, in describing the termination of conflict episodes, we need to address two basic criteria (Vuchinich, 1990). First of all, we need to ask what kind of relationship exists between the penultimate and the final moves in a dispute sequence. Secondly, we need to look at what kind of outcome to the dispute is being decided upon, tacitly or overtly, by the participants. As we will see, on the latter dimension, talk radio disputes have outcomes ranging between "cooperative" and "confrontational" forms. But looking first at the sequential dimension, we find that the sequential environments in which those outcomes are established exhibit patterned features.

The following collection of closing segments illustrates two kinds of patterns. First of all, the final turns of the calls, which are spoken by the host, each consist of two components: an acknowledgment, which takes the general form of "Thank you, [Name]," and then either an address to the audience (extracts [1] and [2]) or the introduction of a next caller (extracts [3], [4], and [5]):

(1) H:21.11.88:14

Caller: I just think that. . .thee:: er, .h methods
of collecting money and so forth, .hh was
just terrific.
Host: Okay thank you very much indeed erm, Myra.
.hh Erm, last warning to take part in the
phone vote. . .

(2) H:21.11.88:6

Host: It's actually not a very difficult thing
to (.) work <u>out</u>.

.hh Thank you very much,
it's: twenty seven and a half past ten.=
Just before the traffic news, .hh erm on:
to this business of whether the Queen
should go: to Moscow. . .

(3) G:26.11.88:3

Host: You'd be much better off if you could in
fact marshal your protests in- in a- in a
more peaceful way but there you are.
Thank you very much Martin,
now Liz of Camberwell. . .

(4) H:21.11.88:9

Host: The system that you introduced was still
charity, it makes no difference.
.hh Thank you Charlie,
Jim:: now good morning.

(5) G:26.11.88:2

Caller: I: think they're dis::gusting.
Host: Uh [thank-]
Caller: [I real]ly do.
Host: Thank you Margaret,
Ma- Martin from Stockwell. . .

In all of these cases, typically for my data corpus, calls are ended unilaterally by the host (in around 120 calls, I found only one example of the caller hanging up on the host). In extracts (1) and (5), the host does this by producing a call-terminal acknowledgment immediately following an evaluative statement by the caller. There is no preclosing sequence by which the here-and-now relevance of a closing might be mutually established, as Schegloff and Sacks (1973) found to be the case for mundane telephone conversations. In extracts (2), (3), and (4), the host's terminal acknowledgment follows an evaluative statement of his own. In these cases, there is an even greater sense of the unilateral nature of the closing moves.

However, the second pattern I referred to is the more interesting one for present purposes. I have noted that, in each case, the "Thank you" is preceded by an evaluative utterance or utterance-component, in short, by an assertion of a speaker's opinion. In extracts (1) and (5), the opinion is the caller's ("I just think [it] was just terrific"; "I: think they're dis::gusting"). In (2), (3), and (4), it is that of the host ("It's actually not a very difficult thing to work out"; "You'd be much better off if you could . . . marshal your protests in a more peaceful way"; "The system that you introduced was still charity it makes no difference"). As noted in chapter 3, position-taking evaluations and assessments such as these may be termination-relevant (Drew & Holt, 1988; C. Goodwin & M. H. Goodwin, 1990; Heritage & Greatbatch, 1986; Schiffrin, 1985). Such devices thus enable the host to link his judgment of when to terminate a call to his judgment of when a call's spate of topical debate or dispute can appropriately (or relevantly) be terminated.[1]

In this way, the end of a call is arrived at with what can somehow be established as the end of the argument that has been carried on during it. However, the end of the argument does not necessarily mean the *resolution* of that argument (as Eisenberg & Garvey, 1981, suggest, for instance). We have seen in the cases shown so far that terminal moves can follow overtly contentious, as opposed to conciliatory, assertions. In this sense, terminating the call can itself operate as a move in an argument.

I now want to look at how these terminal moves function to project particular kinds of outcomes for the disputes they operate to close down. Different types of outcome are connected in various ways to what I describe as cooperative or confrontational terminal segments. The issues raised in the following sections center around the role that closings play in the management of arguments between hosts and callers, and how the asymmetrical technological framework for interaction can have its effects in, and be used as a resource in, the ways that terminal turns are designed.

---

[1]It is interesting to note that a precisely similar pattern can be seen in the single case I have found of a caller unilaterally initiating termination of a conflict episode:

G:3.2.89:9

Caller: Women are very like that Geoffrey I'm a
woman myself I know them they don't like
(0.3) members of their sex to be highly
successful.
Host: Mm hm[:.
Caller: [They just don't like it they're
very jealous creatures.
(.)
Host: .pt Well:,=
Caller: =And- and- and as I said, (0.2) th- the:y
you know they say these things=fancy saying
Missis Thatcher is totally inhuman. (0.3)
That's nonsense. (0.3) Absolute nonsense=
h=That's a:ll I've got to say Geoffrey
thank you ve:y much,
Host: Ye(y) all right thank you very much Jessica
an' an:d we go to Alan...

Again, the termination of the call, carried through this time by the caller, immediately follows a strong assertion of her opinion: "That's nonsense. Absolute nonsense." Further, the caller's final sentence, "That's a:ll I've got to say Geoffrey thank you ve:y much," nicely embodies the next point made in the text, that the end of the call is relevant once the end of the argument, what there is to say on the matter, has been established.

"COOPERATIVE" CALL CLOSINGS

By cooperative closings, I refer to cases in which calls end on a note of assent between caller and host. In one sort of cooperative closing, the host manages the call's termination in such a way that he lets the caller have the last say. In a second type, the last say is taken by the host, but his final turn at least formally takes the shape of an agreement with the caller's position.

Letting the Caller Have the Last Say

In one set of closings, the host ends the call with a simple acknowledgment, "Thank you, [Name]," following a position-statement by the caller:

(1) H:21.11.88:14

1	Host:	An' did you think the same of the telethon
2		when that was on th⌈e one on I-
3	Caller:	⌊I beg your pardon?
4	Host:	Did you think the same of the I.T.V one?
5		(0.8)
6	Caller:	E::r I'm talki- Yes:. (0.5) Yes. I- I- I
7		just think that the e:r, the spirit behind
8		it, an' the way er people 'ave thought of
9		er thee:: er, .h methods of collecting
10		money and so forth, .hh was just terrific.
11→	Host:	Okay thank you very much indeed erm,
12		Myra. .hh Erm, last warnin:g to take part
13		in the phone vote. . .

(5) G:26.11.88:2

1	Caller:	it's really it is the poor, the poorer
2		pensioners that've had it taken away from
3		them. (0.4) Because of this er money
4		that's been e:r the means allowance money.
5	Host:	So you don't think the government's being
6		all that marvelous and generous about
7		th⌈is.
8	Caller:	⌊I: think they're dis::gusting.
9→	Host:	Uh ⌈thank-⌉
10	Caller:	⌊I real⌋ly do.
11→	Host:	Thank you Margaret, Mar-Martin from
12		Stockwell. . .

In these two cases, the caller's point of view, that telethons are "just terrific" (in [1]) or the government is "dis::gusting" (in [5]), ends up acting as the last word in the call. By terminating the call with a simple acknowledgment, the host adds nothing to, and does not detract from, the caller's statement of opinion, but moves straight away to the next caller.

One thing to note, however, is the way that the host, in both cases, appears to create an environment for a cooperative call closing by doing a cooperative action in the turn preceding the caller's final turn. In extract (1), the caller had been extolling the virtues of telethons. The host's question in line 4 is cooperative in that it presents the caller with the chance to continue extolling, this time by reference to a different telethon. And after a brief confusion (with "E::r I'm talki-" at the beginning of line 6, the caller seems to be about to say "I'm talking about that one"), she emphatically agrees (line 6) and accepts the invitation to go on in a similar vein.

In extract (5), the cooperative action on the host's part consists of him summarizing the caller's point in lines 5–7: "So you don't think the government's being all that marvelous and generous about this." As Heritage and Watson (1979) have pointed out, such summarizing formulations can operate as moves in bringing discussions to a close. The host's formulation, by offering a version of the argument to which the caller can readily assent, sets up a cooperative environment in which the call can be ended, once again, on the caller's emphatic assertion of her opinion.

A slightly different kind of case is provided in extract (6). The caller has been arguing against a prior caller's objection to what the latter saw as a biased TV documentary about the death of a suspect in police custody. (The prior caller had complained at how the program showed "the mother crying," and made much of the fact that the victim had been "in the Boys Brigade movement." This call is reproduced as extract [10] later.)

(6) H:30.11.88:8

Caller:	But all we saw was a woman's grief,
Host:	Okay well erm::,=
Caller:	=A[nd an ordin]ar[y y]oung man who was=
Host:	[Yi- yi-] [Yeh]
Caller:	=in the boy scou[ts and who was >°whatever
Host:	[Right I understand,
	I understand Ivy and er understand m- the
	point you're making particularly fr- from
	the your starting point which was that .hh
	you will see .hh controversial programmes
	from .hh a particular (.) point of view,
	.hhh and we've had two of those particular
	points of views, .h er yours and earlier
	Steven's. Thank you very much indeed for
	calling us, to Morris next in Tooting. . .

Here, the host makes a move to close the call in line 2.[2] But this is cut into by

[2]See Schegloff and Sacks (1973) on how "Okay" is used as a preclosing move.

the caller as she adds further components in her assessment of the TV show's treatment of its topic. Following this, the host cuts back in with a second try for a termination (line 6). Only here, prior to closing the call with the standard "Thank you," he himself produces a summary of the caller's point. Notice, however, that the summary actually *selects* from the caller's argument a particular point: "particularly . . . your starting point which was that you will see controversial programmes from a particular . . . point of view" (lines 8–11). What we find here, then, is a more selective form of agreement. The host allows a viewpoint put by the caller to act as the last word in the call, but uses his selection of that particular point to formulate his own assenting view. It is noticeable, in this regard, that his abandoned closing attempt in line 2, "Okay well erm," presages this selective agreement, in that one routine use of the discourse marker "Well" is as a preface to a disagreement (Pomerantz, 1984a).

Host Agrees With the Caller

In a second group of cooperative closings, the utterance immediately preceding the terminal "Thank you" is one in which the host expresses an opinion on his own behalf, though one in which at least formally he agrees with the caller's point of view.

A relatively straightforward case is provided in extract (7), where the topic of the call is a proposed official visit by the Queen to what was then the Soviet Union. The caller supports such a visit, and opposes those who object on such grounds as the Soviet Union's lax record on human rights.

(7) H:21.11.88:16

Caller: I mean there could be:, e:r there's lots
of other countries which ha:ve er records
which, .hh you know don't- aren't clean
all the time ei:ther. But, .hh I- I
think e:r something like, the Queen going
over there could be good. An[d .hh
Host: [Yes I s'pose
if we do use the argument of human rights
it erm, leaves very few countries, in:
the wor:ld that would be: erm, good enough
for the Queen to visit. .hh Thank you
Gary,

Note that the final turn of the call, which again follows an evaluative assertion by the caller (lines 5–6), begins with the host assenting to the caller's view. It then proceeds to a termination with no intervening talk from the caller. But in this case, the host is not proposing to formulate a position expressed by the caller, as in extract (6), but is more overtly expressing a stance on his own behalf that is in agreement with the caller. That agreement is not necessarily wholehearted, however. There is a sense in which his use of the phrase "I suppose" in line 7 signals some form of concession to the caller's point. Nevertheless, although it is not the caller who has the last say, the call ends with no argumentative residue between the participants.

Extract (8) presents a slightly different phenomenon. Once again, the last turn of the call consists of a lengthy utterance in which the host moves from an expression of agreement with the caller to a termination with no intervening talk. However, in agreeing with the caller, the host does more than the kind of straightforward if grudging assent that we found in extract (7):

(8) H:21.11.88:7

Caller: Of course if all of us could claim er a
tax deduction, .h for any charitable
donation, .h I think it's a fair point to
suggest that erm (.) the country in
general terms=.h=or charities in general
terms, .h would get massive (.) e:r sums
coming .h e:r coming in:, .h which don't
come in now.
Host: Yes it would be a way that thee (.)
government could help .hh e::rm the- the
sick and the poor=I'm just trying to m-
(.) .hh yihknow put it into a cun- uhn f-
a convenient phrase, but without
necessarily doing it itself. Now that
would go against the argument that was
put .h by an earlier caller that there
shouldn't be any charity collecting at all
anyway because the .hhh government should
provide the money. .hh Thank you Bill,
Peter in Lewisham next. . .

Beginning in line 9, the host puts forward an assenting position, which nonetheless places a different emphasis from the caller's on the point in question. Instead of focusing on the extra amounts of money that tax-deductible charitable donations would generate, he focuses on how such a policy would allow the government to help "the sick and the poor" without legislating to turn charitable organizations into state-funded bodies. This way of putting it allows him to pit this argument against an earlier caller's position (lines 14–19), with which he had strongly disagreed. Thus, the host's agreement here has an orientation to disagreement or controversy superimposed upon it, in that it is used to carry on his dispute with the prior caller.

The cases presented in this section can all be described as cooperative because, broadly speaking, the relationship between the final turns in the terminal segment is one of assent rather than opposition. Closing moves instigated by the host follow upon position statements by callers; but whether the closing turns take the form of simple acknowledgments, or take an alternative format in which the host's own opinion plays a larger role, the host does not take issue with the stance of the caller at hand.

Nonetheless, in terms of the call's outcome, some of these cases (such as extract [8]) show an orientation not only to agreement but also to argument and/or controversy. In this sense, the policy of agreeing with the caller at hand can in fact be used in a wider pursuit of controversy in the issues and themes being discussed.

CONFRONTATIONAL CLOSINGS: THE "POWER OF THE LAST WORD"

We have already seen that arguments may end on a note of opposition rather than assent between the participants. In these cases, the pattern is that the host's negation of the caller's stance comes in a position-taking utterance of his own, which occupies the entire terminal segment. This is illustrated by extract (9), in which the final turn of the call shows the host first dissenting from the caller's view, then directly moving to a terminal acknowledgment:

(9) H:21.11.88:11

Caller: . . .what I think is that these telethons
are educating people but they're educating
them in a certain way they're educating
them to give money. What they should be
doing is educating them to take an
interest in their community. .hh Instead
of just giving money which can in fact,
.hh stop them being interested [because-
Host: [Well I
don't think the job of the telethon is to
educate people to do anything, .h er it
gives them an opportunity, .mhh e:r
through a kind of entertainment if you
like, .hhh to give money. Now you may
not like that, .hh I don't find it,
terribly entertaining to watch, .hh but I
certainly wouldn't prevent people who do
enjoy it, .hhh er from seeing it, .h being
entertained and at the same time giving
money, .h whether it salves consciousnes-
uh consciences or not. .hh Thank you
Philip, .hh it's: er twelve minutes to
eleven. . .

The host's turn begins as a straightfoward disagreement with the caller's position that telethons are "educating people" in the wrong kind of way: "Well I don't think the job of the telethon is to educate people to do anything." Subsequently, he puts his own dissenting view on the matter, before ultimately closing the call with a terminal "Thank you," leaving no space for a rejoinder from the caller. In this kind of case, the sense of confrontation is promoted in terms of both the relationship between the final turns of the call and the disputatious nature of the call's conclusion itself. In having the last say in the call, the host thereby gains the last say in an ongoing dispute over the issue.

Clearly, hosts are in a very powerful position for having the last say in their disputes with callers. In an important sense, that power is connected to the technological framework within which hosts and callers interact. By virtue of the technologically mediated nature of talk radio disputes, the host has at his disposal a specific resource for not allowing the caller an opportunity to respond to his last word. That is, he can close off the caller's channel of access to the argumentative arena while retaining full access to that arena himself.

But as I have argued before, the power that is attached to the interactional and technological arrangements of talk radio does not come into play as an automatic effect. It exists only as potentialities that must be instantiated in actual talk.[3] The way in which the "power of the last word" can be instantiated as an interactional resource is illustrated particularly clearly in the examples that follow.

In the call from which the next extract was taken, the caller has complained that a TV program about the death of a suspect in police custody was "biased" against the police. The host has developed the position that the program had a particular perspective on the subject and so was inevitably selective in its presentation of the "facts." In the extract, the host's attempts to take a counter-position are repeatedly overlapped by the caller doggedly pursuing his own line (lines 6, 8, and 15). The host responds by verbally closing down the caller's channel of access using a terminal acknowledgment in order to put his own point forward (line 20):

(10) H:30.11.88:5

Host: But you do have to come to your own
conclusion when you watch things, .hh erm
quite often things are biased the other
way, .phh e:r you know the- the the- (.)
.ph consta[ntly put opinion] that=
Caller: [I: just fail-]
Host: =[[the police are] won[derful]
Caller: [[u:h a:-absolu] [I fai]l to see

[3]As I observe in more detail in the concluding chapter, this model of power is strikingly close to that developed on a more theoretical plane by Foucault (1977).

9 what- what 'is antecedence in the church
10 'ad anything to do with it. Or or [or i]s=
11 Host: [Well,]
12 Caller: =it in the Boys Brigade
13 movemen[t.
14 Host: [Yeh [but that's understandable.]
15 Caller: [.hhh an' they kep' show]in'
16 you the funeral the mother cryin' .hh th-
17 the everybody wailin' over the grave I mean
18 i- was totally unnecessary.
20 Host: Okay Steven thank you very much indeed,
21 erm:, it is understandable how- however if
22 you, bi- have the ki:nd of view that
23 you're suggesting that programme (.) had,
24 .hhmhh e:::rm, that they should e:rm, .hh
25 (.) talk about thee- the character, of the
26 victim. .thh Thank you Steven, a::nd
27 Gerald, good morning. . .

In line 6, the caller interrupts the host's attempt to argue against his line that the program was biased against the police and, having gained the floor (line 8), pursues his line of complaint. The host then appears to make another attempt at arguing (line 11), but the "Well" that signals this attempt is overlapped as the caller adds yet another sentence onto his complaint. A further attempt is made in line 14, but this too is overlapped by the caller as he adds yet more points to his complaint. In his final attempt to put his view forward, however, the host precedes the resumption of his argument with a terminal acknowledgment, "thank you very much indeed" (line 20).

We thus see how, faced with a recalcitrant caller with whom he wants to disagree, the host may deploy the strategy of getting in the last word *after* he has closed the call. The significance of this is that no comparable strategy is available to the caller. Although callers may elect to terminate a call unilaterally, they can do so only by withdrawing from the interactional arena, and therefore withdrawing from the argument. Vuchinich (1990) has shown that withdrawing is one among a small number of strategies by which participants in conversational arguments terminate disputes. By physically leaving the arena, a participant may seek to kill the dispute by effectively leaving his or her codisputant no one to argue with. But when the dispute takes place in public, as on talk radio, withdrawing can be a disadvantageous strategy, because the upshot is not that one gets the last word oneself, but that the last word is thereby ceded to one's opponent.

On talk radio, this feature is compounded by the asymmetry in the participants' levels of technical access to the public arena. The host's institutional status is supported by a technological positioning which enables him, if he so chooses, to have the last word in a dispute by expressing his opinion in a public space that is not available to the caller: the space occurring after the caller's channel of access to the host and the audience has been closed down, either by the host himself, or by the caller hanging up on the host.

Although this claim sounds quite plausible, a possible empirical problem is that the recorded data on which these analyses are based do not in themselves provide evidence that would allow us to say at what point the caller's access to the air may actually have been closed off. In other words, in the absence of additional ethnographic data, it is not clear to what extent callers may be complying with the host's getting the last word by remaining silent, as opposed to *being* silenced by virtue of being cut off.[4]

That lack of ethnographic data may be seen as a significant absence, given the concern of this chapter with the endings and outcomes of arguments on talk radio.[5] However, the data at hand—recordings and transcripts of the actual broadcast talk—can in fact provide their own kind of evidence that allows us to see how the asymmetry in channels of access is used as a resource by the host in accomplishing the termination of calls and of arguments. One sort of evidence for this is provided by the previous extract, in which we saw the host using the routine closing device of "Thank you, [Name]" *before* putting forward his own position. In that call, the technological asymmetry between host and caller is actively utilized by the former to win out in a dispute.

A second type of evidence we can look at consists of cases where callers remain on the air during the host's closing move, and attempt to resist that move. In these cases, the host unilaterally closes the call on an oppositional note by overriding the caller's objections and pushing through to a termination. In extract (11), the caller had earlier proposed a system aimed at superseding charitable donations, based on a personal tax levied by the government that would then be distributed to the various organizations currently reliant on charitable giving. As the extract begins, the caller has moved on to complain about the number of mailed requests for donations that he claims to receive from such organizations:

[4]During observational visits to a studio to watch a talk radio show in progress, it was clear to me that the host did indeed sometimes close down callers' channels before he had closed the call by acknowledging their contribution. But because no ethnographic notes exist that correlate with the particular recordings I made (the recorded data were collected much earlier than these visits), the problem referred to in this paragraph remains.

[5]This is a claim that would no doubt be supported by Cicourel (1981), who argues that recorded data must be supplemented by ethnographic data drawn from fieldnotes and interviews if we are to fully understand the relationship between interactional processes and social institutions. Such a view is not held by conversation analysts, for two reasons. First, as outlined in chapter 1, institutions are constituted in and through the details of interaction that can best be observed in the form of relative specializations in the design and exchange of turns. Second, that level of interaction, which CA reveals, is largely tacit, and so it is not clear what analytic status additional interview data would have. Such data would be additional, but only in the sense that they deal with social action at a quite different level.

(11) H:21.11.88:9

1	Caller:	But then a'course y- you <u>do</u> get eventually
2		you find yourself about thirty or forty
3		different charities comin' through your
4		post an' you can't donate to <u>all</u> of them.
5		.hhh It's such an ex<u>pen</u>se isn' it when
6		people .hhh [these ( ) send out
7	Host:	[Well you don't haff- n-a- hold
8		<u>o</u>:n, a m- a moment ag<u>o</u>: you were saying we
9		should give to <u>all</u> of them, now you're
10		saying .h it's too <u>diff</u>icult to give to
11		them, .h e[r the s:-
12	Caller:	[N- no [the-
13	Host:	[the <u>sys</u>tem that you
14		introduced [was still] charity it makes no=
16	Caller:	[It ( )]
17	Host:	=<u>diff</u>erence. .hh Thank you Charlie, J<u>i</u>m::
18		now good morning.

In lines 7–10 the host begins by arguing that the caller's line has become incoherent: "a moment ag<u>o</u>: you were saying we should give to all of them, now you're saying it's too <u>diff</u>icult to give to them." Notice, however, that the caller begins to take issue with this characterization of what he is saying (line 12). But the host holds the floor through this attempted objection, going on to state his opposition to the caller's principal point. In the process, he talks over a second apparent objection by the caller (line 16), and ultimately, terminates the call on this expression of his opposing line (line 17).

Similar features can be seen in extract (12):

(12) G:26.11.88:10

1	Host:	I see you- you- you're going back to the
2		ol:d- the old argument that people have too
3		many children and therefore that
4		imp<u>o</u>verishes them are you?
5		(0.3)
6	Caller:	.hh <u>Well</u> I [think-
7	Host:	[Not a very enlightened view I
8		would've thought, [but perha- per]haps=
9	Caller:	[.hh <u>No</u> no:.]
10	Host:	=perhaps you come from the fortunate
11		minority Marjorie=th[ank you very muh-]=
12	Caller:	[No<u>:</u> I d<u>o</u>:n't,]
13	Host:	=.h Th<u>a</u>nk you very much we go to Mabel. . .

The host attributes a position to the caller in the first turn of the extract. But once it is clear that the caller is about to take issue with some aspect of that attribution (as signaled in lines 5 and 6 through the slight pause and the disagreement marker, "Well"), he interrupts her (line 7), again overriding further objections from the caller (line 9 and line 12), before ultimately terminating the call.

In sum, asymmetries in participant status that are connected to the technological asymmetries of talk radio become a resource available to the host for accomplishing confrontational closings. Even in the absence of additional data that tell us whether or not callers' lines of access have actually been closed down, we find empirical evidence of hosts utilizing that access asymmetry in order to determine the public outcome of a dispute. In examples where hosts observably work to blot out objections from callers, strong evidence is provided of how the potential power dynamic in this context is actually instantiated in the local practices of talking.

CONCLUSION

The observations made in this chapter serve to highlight the relevance of the public arena in which talk radio disputes are carried out. The asymmetries outlined here arise as a result of the participants' unequal access to that public arena, populated by the overhearing audience. This adds a further dimension to my analysis of power relations in talk radio discourse, because it illustrates that power, on talk radio, is not just a phenomenon linked to and produced through the sequential details of talk, but is also connected in significant ways to the mediated nature of the interaction. The outcomes of talk radio disputes, the determination of which we have observed in this chapter, are public outcomes, in the sense that the last word is a *broadcast* word.[6] Clearly, there is a sense in which callers could have the last word on their own terms, by continuing to argue with the host's voice on the radio after their call has ended. But the relevance of arguments on talk radio is precisely that they take place in the public sphere of broadcasting, and this represents a principal reason for callers to place a call in the first place (Rancer et al., 1994).

As I have suggested throughout the book, by orienting to particular patterns of conduct, participants in institutional encounters become involved in

---

[6]Although I have argued that callers, by hanging up, effectively cede this last broadcast word to the host, it is of course possible that the host may choose not to use that opportunity to have the last say in an argument. In fact, the only case I have located in my data corpus, reproduced in footnote 1 of this chapter, is just such a case. There, after the caller has hung up, saying, "That's a:ll I've got to say Geoffrey thank you ve:y much," the host responds simply by saying, "all right thank you," and moves on to the next caller. The point, however, is once again that the host has a different range of possibilities open to him than the caller does. In this example, the host *could* have argued back, whereas the caller has denied herself the possibility of responding to any further potential rejoinder.

the reproduction of a power dynamic, which is instantiated in discourse. As this chapter has shown, in the case of calls on talk radio, a significant factor is that the host may set the temporal boundaries of the caller's participation in the public arena, and so determine what will count as the outcome of a dispute. Of course, as with all forms of power, there are means of resistance available. But the caller's main means of resistance to these powerful strategies (i.e., hanging up) ultimately backfires, because in the talk show's relevant public context, all such a strategy achieves is to provide the host with an open opportunity to take the floor, and at least appear to have won the dispute.

7 Conclusion

This book has had two principal aims. First, I wanted to describe the kinds of argumentative resources available to and used by talk radio hosts and callers to engage in confrontation talk. Second, I wanted to explore the relationship between the verbal and interactive practices of arguing and the institutional features of the talk radio show, as a social setting in which arguments routinely take place. The book's empirical chapters have shown how the sequential orientation of conversation analysis can be used to address this issue. In doing so, we have seen how conversation analysis, which traditionally has avoided making claims about power relations in discourse, can in fact be used to address that issue in a highly contextually and interactionally sensitive way.

INSTITUTIONAL DIMENSIONS OF TALK RADIO DISCOURSE

At the heart of the book has been a complex web of relationships between the interactional processes of argument, the institutional processes of talk radio, and the play of power and its resistance in argumentative discourse. I began by developing a general framework in which arguments could be analyzed as dynamic interactional accomplishments. The Action–Opposition sequence described in chapter 2 represented a model for analyzing not only how arguments emerge out of contingent oppositions to arguable actions, but also how arguments are sustained by the chaining of Action–Opposition sequences.

Applying this model to arguments on talk radio, the chapter showed that, like conversation, talk radio disputes involve a relatively unconstrained exchange of personal opinions. But at the same time, those disputes are constrained in various ways by certain institutional imperatives and systematic asymmetries. These constraints differ from the distinctive sequential constraints that operate in formal institutional styles of dispute, such as those found in courtrooms, news interviews, and dispute mediation settings. Although the activities engaged in by participants in these settings are themselves specialized, the principal way in which the institutional character of the interaction has been analyzed is in terms of specialized turn-taking systems in which turn forms like questioning and answering are linked to, and instantiate, given institutional identities (Heritage & Greatbatch, 1991). On talk radio, on the other hand, the turn-taking style is far more conversational. Consequently, disputes derive their asymmetrical properties principally from the organization of specific activities within calls (i.e., the activities of stating an opinion and skeptically challenging or disagreeing with it).

Subsequent chapters linked the structures of talk-in-interaction with the participation structures provided by the organization of talk radio calls. Chapters 3, 4, and 5 located connections between the use of particular argumentative devices and the participants' respective positions within the overall activity framework of the call. Some of these devices and resources were seen to be differentially available to the host and the caller. For instance, the validity challenges and formulations described in chapter 3 appear to be almost exclusively hosts' resources. Similarly, the "You say (X)" device which was the focus of chapter 4 represents a resource used exclusively by the host in my data collection. And in my discussion of interruptive strategies in chapter 5, I noted that certain of these strategies, such as post-response-initiation interruptions, are used virtually entirely by hosts and not by callers. All these asymmetries were related to a crucial feature of talk radio interaction: the fact that it is the caller's task to present an opinion and the host's job to react to what the caller says.

These observations enabled me to address the central theme of the book: the relationship between talk radio as an institution, interactional asymmetry, and power. I argued that this relationship can be traced in the details of talk, and specifically in the connections between the organization of activities within calls, and the asymmetrical distribution of argument resources. Most importantly, in chapter 3, I showed how the opening of the call is not only designed to set up an environment in which callers get to introduce their topics, but by virtue of that, it places the participants on significantly asymmetrical footings with respect to those topics. The fact that callers are required, and can be constrained, to go first by expressing a point of view on some issue means that hosts systematically get to go second.

However, my aim was not just to note that asymmetry. Going second, I argued, represents a more powerful position in argumentative discourse than going first. I analyzed how that power operates to enable the host to critique or attack the caller's line simply by exhibiting skepticism about its claims, challenging the agenda-relevance of assertions, or taking the argument apart by identifying minor inaccuracies in its details.

Of course, the fact that hosts *may* conduct arguments without expressing a counterposition or providing explanations and accounts for their own positions does not mean that they never do this. The point is that hosts are in a position to do this whereas callers, purely by virtue of the organization of the call, are not. At the same time, I noted numerous ways in which there are resources available for callers to resist the host's powerful strategies, and sometimes to exercise powerful strategies themselves. Thus, power has not been viewed as a monolithic, institutionalized feature of talk radio. Although it is true that the host is "in control of the mechanics of the radio program" (Moss & Higgins, 1984, p. 373), the power dynamics that operate within, and are instantiated through, the talk itself are variable and shifting, and the host's power of the "last word," described in chapter 6, is only one part of that.

The empirical analyses, then, have been addressed to a set of broader themes. One of them is how talk radio functions as an institution that is both constituted by, and at the same time places specific constraints on, the practices of talk-in-interaction carried out by its participants. This links the book into a wider sociological literature that is concerned with the relationship between interaction and social structure. It is necessary now to summarize where the book stands in relation to that theoretical issue. Second, a key question has been that of how power is instantiated in discourse. The explicitness of that emphasis represents a relatively new dimension in conversation analytic work on talk in institutional settings. Consequently, the model of power that has emerged from these empirical analyses also needs to be outlined in a more systematic way.

INTERACTION AND SOCIAL STRUCTURE

Key to much recent work on institutional discourse has been the idea that interaction and the social structural contexts represented by institutional settings are reflexively related, rather than existing at distinct levels which compete for analytic attention. To use the terms introduced by Giddens (1981), some conventional institutional theorists (e.g., Blau, 1987) still want to view interaction and social structure as competing poles of a duality. Others, however, argue that the details of interaction and the features of social structure are intrinsically and reflexively related, so that one cannot be understood without reference to the other (e.g., Cicourel, 1981; Fairclough, 1989; Giddens, 1984). As Giddens (1981) puts it, the two can more profitably be seen as complementary poles of a duality.

Giddens' (1984) idea of the "duality of structure" is perhaps the most extensively worked out theoretical expression of this approach. The notion of the duality of structure maintains that "social structures are both constituted *by* human agency and yet at the same time are the very *medium* of this constitution" (Giddens, 1976, p. 121). In other words, structural aspects of society both operate as resources for, and are products of, social interaction. We cannot adequately understand the large-scale phenomena that institutional theorists have studied without explicit reference to the actual, local practices of social interaction through which such structures are brought into being, and without which they could not exist. But at the same time, interaction does not take place in an institutional vacuum, and neither are institutional phenomena created anew on each new interactional occasion. Past practices and regularities, embedded and embodied in culture and memory, inform people's actions, whereas those actions in turn recursively recreate (while also potentially changing) the institutional frameworks that we observe both in the vernacular and in the macrosociological sense.

When conversation analysts turn to look at institutional data, they adopt a position that is very close to this, although it is typically not articulated on the theoretical level. Rather, CA seeks to describe how the recursivity of action and structure operates on the empirical level, by examining talk-in-interaction. The position taken by CA is, broadly, this: If structure informs talk, and talk simultaneously constitutes structure, then those processes cannot simply be theoretically prescribed; they must be observable in the details of talk itself (Schegloff, 1991).

A good deal of conversation analytic work in this area has now been done (see especially the collections in Boden & Zimmerman, 1991, and Drew & Heritage, 1992). However, the main question addressed in this work has been that of the constitution of institutional settings through the variety of specialized turn-taking systems and other design features of talk-in-interaction that have been described. As Drew and Heritage (1992) point out in their introduction to this range of work, at the heart of most of it has been a concern with how question–answer sequences are configured in specialized ways in almost all examples of institutional discourse. Less attention has been paid to the other side of the reflexive coin: the question of how institutional interaction frameworks function to distribute verbal resources asymmetrically so that different categories of participants end up with significantly different interactional prerogatives.

It is this latter issue that has been at the core of my analyses of talk radio in this book. I have suggested that there is a reflexive relationship between the interactional practices through which the talk radio context is constituted, on the one hand, and the asymmetric interactional frameworks within which participants are situated, on the other. The way in which calls are structured through participants' practices in turn opens up a distinctive field of possibilities for each participant to conduct him or herself in relation to the other.

This claim has not been based on specialized features of question–answer adjacency pairs, but on the way in which the interactive resources and sequential structures of argument operate within the specific configuration of activities that characterizes calls on talk radio. At the heart of this has been the relationship between first and second positions and their associated arrays of resources. At root, my position has been that these are structurally asymmetrical arrays, which is to say that they have to do not with the features of particular arguments, but with the properties of argument per se.

This means that whereas the organizational pattern of talk radio calls is initially constituted through (and *only* through) the participants' routine ways of conducting calls, that organizational pattern simultaneously situates the participants in a structurally asymmetrical relationship. This version of the reflexive relationship between interaction and structural aspects of social settings has been applied specifically to talk radio in the present book; but that does not mean that the same approach would not apply to other forms of institutional discourse. Indeed, as I outlined in chapter 1, a great many conversation-analytic studies of institutional interaction seem to imply such a position very strongly. By focusing on how participants display an orientation to institutional settings by selectively engaging in certain activities and refraining from others, CA is involved in showing how participants not only constitute, but also become structurally constrained by, the differential distributions of resources that are associated with such oriented-to activity patterns.

In this book, I have used that approach to advance some claims about the play of power in institutional discourse. I have shown how an asymmetrical distribution of resources emerges as a result of the sequential organization of calls on talk radio. I have also argued that it is in these sequential environments that the play of power, and its resistance, emerges as an observable phenomenon in the talk. These claims have been based not only on a particular way of thinking about the relationship between action and structure, but also on a particular way of conceptualizing power.

POWER RELATIONS IN DISCOURSE

In the preceding chapters, I have used the idea of a relationship between activities and organizational structures as the basis for developing an account of the play of power in calls on talk radio. In doing so, I have argued that power is a phenomenon brought into play through discourse. I have focused on relatively small sequential details of arguments in order to illustrate this idea.

What I have attempted, broadly speaking, is the application of the sequential approach developed within conversation analysis to a question that has concerned critical linguists and discourse analysts (i.e., how power operates in and through language) by viewing power in terms of the relationships between turns in sequences.

Power is an issue on which conversation analysts have tended to remain agnostic. Perhaps because it is, at root, a value-laden vernacular concept, or possibly because it is a term deeply associated with the kind of "conventional sociology" against which ethnomethodological approaches have traditionally ranged themselves, power is not a term that CA typically employs. Even when researchers analyze institutional data that clearly show differential distributions of verbal resources between particular social identities, reports favor the more neutral term "asymmetry." For instance, in the index to Drew and Heritage's (1992) collection of papers on institutional interaction, there are only 4 listings for "power" (and 3 of those refer to a critical discussion of social scientific uses of the concept by Schegloff), yet there are 18 references for "interactional asymmetries."

When CA-oriented researchers do write about structural asymmetries, the relationship between these and power as an interactional process is rarely addressed. Exceptions here are Davis' (1988) study of doctor–patient consultations, and Watson's (1990) analysis of the elicitation of confessions in police suspect interrogations. In both these studies, power is taken as a central issue. Watson's (1990) principal concern is to show that power cannot be read off as a feature of objectively existing relationships between participants (e.g., police officer and suspect). Rather, power "must be firmly located in the systematic examination of features integral to the discourse itself" (p. 280). Davis (1988), on the other hand, argues that although a CA approach can be used to address power relations between doctors and patients, in order to do so adequately it needs to incorporate a much more detailed theoretical underpinning deriving from the work of Giddens.

In this book, I have recognized the relevance of that theoretical work, but the main emphasis has been on empirical investigation of how power operates and is instantiated in the integral features of discourse. On the basis of empirical analysis of turn formats and turn sequences, I have shown that we can address power as a phenomenon that is both highly specific, and also diffusely and pervasively present within an interaction.

The model of power that thereby emerges is closely related to elements of the theoretical conception outlined by Foucault (1977). Foucault's view of power treats it not as a zero-sum game in which a finite amount of social power gets distributed among social agents and groupings, but instead as a set of potentials which, although always present, can be varyingly exercised, resisted, shifted around, and struggled over by social agents. Foucault argues that power is not a thing that is possessed by one agent or collectivity and lacked by another, but a practice that is exercised within a relational network equally including those who exercise power and those who accept or resist it. The network itself is viewed as a structure of possibilities and not as a concrete relationship between determinate social entities.

Foucault's work is often pitched at the broadest theoretical level, and his ideas about power extend far beyond this starting point. Principally, Foucault argues that certain "discourses" or modes of rhetoric and reasoning embody and reproduce power relationships within society. For example, the technical medical discourses relied on by doctors reproduces the power of the medical profession over patients (see Silverman, 1987). However, although it is emphasized that this power of discourses can be resisted using other discourses, it is often unclear precisely what empirical status such discourses have. Of course, discourses are only ever instantiated in talk (or in other actual forms of language use, such as written documents). But Foucault's interest in the form and function of the manifold discourses by which we make sense of ourselves, others, and the world in which we are situated leads his research away from the micro details of interaction and toward the larger spans of history traced in archive documents.

For this reason, although my notion of power is related to Foucault's, it is also very different. In thinking about power in this book I have focused entirely on talk. Most specifically, I have described the ways in which the organization of participation in the talk radio setting, which is always the local accomplishment of the participants as they talk, can have unintended consequences in terms of their differential capabilities to act or constrain the other from acting. First and second positions are structural features of argument, which have definite consequences for the conduct of a dispute. These positions can be struggled over in any dispute, but on talk radio the way calls are organized leads to the host initially taking (and subsequently being in a better position to maintain) second position against the caller. Thus, whether the participants intend it or not, a form of power relationship is built into the very set of turn-taking practices by which they collaboratively accomplish the call. It is in this sense that I have addressed the relationship between talk and social structure, and the play of power in discourse.

Nevertheless, the empirical analyses in this book go some way toward demonstrating how two of Foucault's central ideas can help in the analysis of power at the interpersonal level, in the details of talk-in-interaction. These ideas are, first, that wherever there is power, there is resistance, and second, that power operates in the most mundane contexts of everyday life, not just at the macro level of large processes (Foucault, 1977).

On resistance, I have stressed throughout that although hosts have a "natural" incumbency in second position, and thereby have available a set of powerful resources for dealing skeptically with callers' contributions, there are ways in which callers may resist those strategies. They may do this by recognizing and attempting somehow to forestall the effects of the powerful strategy being used by the host (as discussed, e.g., in chapter 4). Or they may resist by attempting to adopt the powerful strategies available to the host for themselves, by taking opportunities to move into second position (as discussed in chapter 3).

The second point is perhaps the one with which this book resonates most strongly. There is a tendency in both mundane and social scientific discourse to conceive of power as a "big" phenomenon, operating at the largest scale within social formations. Foucault on the other hand suggests that power is pervasive even at the smallest level of interpersonal relationships. As I have remarked, the kind of power with which Foucault is mainly concerned exists in the form of the ever-shifting discourses that give shape and meaning to the world and our relationships in it. I have focused on a different kind of power: the discursive power that threads through the course and trajectory of an argument. But I have located that form of power among the smallest details of social life: the construction of turns and the relationships between turns in one form of everyday talk.

CONCLUSION

The theoretical connections and implications outlined in this chapter should not blind us to the fact that the book as a whole stands firmly within the methodological framework of conversation analysis. The sequential organization of talk-in-interaction has, of course, been the fundamental focus for CA, and it is that focus that is at the root of CA's distinctive contribution to the study of social interaction. I have used CA to illustrate how there are reflexive connections between the sequential organization of talk, interactional asymmetries, and power in institutional discourse. Although it is true that conversation analysts have tended to be diffident regarding issues of power in interaction, this book has shown that such issues can be addressed without compromising the strong methodological principles that mark CA's distinctive contribution to the study of talk and interaction. Instead of avoiding the issue or claiming that it is something that falls outside CA's empirical range, or arguing that supplementary theoretical instruments need to be brought in to bolster CA's empiricism, I have used the case of talk radio to show how CA is in fact capable of addressing not just the institutional nature of talk, but also the play of power in institutional interaction, on its own terms.

A Appendix A: Transcription Conventions

Underlining	word	Stress
Colons	wo::rd	Extended sound
Left brackets	wo[rd [word	Overlap begins
Right brackets	word] wo]rd	Overlap ends
Equals sign	word=word	Latching
Dot- "h"	.hhh	Audible inbreath
"h"	hhh	Audible outbreath
Bracketed "h"	wor(h)d	Embedded laughter
Degree signs	°word°	Quiet speech
Chevrons	>word<	Speed-up in delivery
Bracketed numbers	(0.0)	Timed pauses
Bracketed dot	(.)	Micropause (< 0.2 second)
Question mark	?	Rising intonation
Comma	,	"Holding" intonation
Period	.	Falling intonation
Dash	wor-	Cut-off or glottal stop
Capitals	WORD	Loud talk

B Appendix B: Use of Data in the Book

I have made use of a wide variety of data sources throughout the book. Although the greatest proportion of data extracts are drawn from my principal source of recordings of talk radio shows, I have used other data sources freely in order to illustrate points, indicate generalizability, or draw contrastive comparisons. In this, I have relied on one of the key characteristics of CA: the fact that its practitioners make their data available to others who wish to pursue related lines of inquiry or to question published analyses.

In all cases, data extracts are identified by a code that appears at the top of the extract and refers to the extract's location in the original researcher's library. In the case of my talk radio data, these codes refer to the name of the host, the date of the broadcast, the call's position in that broadcast's sequence of calls, and the page number of the transcript from which the extract was taken. So a code such as: **H:21.11.88:6:2** shows that the host was Brian Hayes (note that there are two individuals who hosted the broadcasts in my data corpus, the other being **G**, George Goodman), the show was broadcast on **21.11.88** (note that I use the British convention of putting the month second), the call was number **6** in the show, and the page number is **2**.

Other codes refer to other researchers' sources. For instance, **WAO** is a British radio news program; **NB**, **TRIO**, and **SBL** are sets of telephone conversations between friends recorded in the United States (although with the exception of **TRIO** the corpora are large and participants within them vary); **BC** refers to a collection of recordings of an American talk radio show; **SCC** comes from recordings of hearings in a British small claims court; and **GTS** refers to a series of group therapy sessions involving teenagers and a therapist in his 30s.

The specific type of situation in which data extracts were recorded is frequently indicated in the text: That is, I refer to extracts as "from a news interview" or "from ordinary conversation." Where an extract is taken from the talk radio materials, this is made additionally clear because the participants are designated "Host" and "Caller," respectively. It should be stressed that the supplementary data sources have been used only illustratively, and not as the basis for my analyses. However, where data has been made available to me by a specific individual, that person has been acknowledged in a footnote.

References

Atkinson, J. M. (1984a). *Our masters' voices: The language and body language of politics*. London: Methuen.

Atkinson, J. M. (1984b). Public speaking and audience response: Some techniques for inviting applause. In J. M. Atkinson & J. Heritage (Eds.), *Structures of social action: Studies in conversation analysis* (pp. 370–409). Cambridge: Cambridge University Press.

Atkinson, J. M., & Drew, P. (1979). *Order in court: The organization of verbal interaction in judicial settings*. London: Macmillan.

Avery, R., & Ellis, D. (1979). Talk radio as an interpersonal phenomenon. In G. Gumpert & C. Cathcart (Eds.), *Inter/Media* (pp. 108–115). New York: Oxford University Press.

Beattie, G. (1983). *Talk: Analysis of speech and non-verbal behavior in conversation*. Milton Keynes: Open University Press.

Bergmann, J. (1992). Veiled morality: Notes on discretion in psychiatry. In P. Drew & J. Heritage (Eds.), *Talk at work: Interaction in institutional settings* (pp. 137–162). Cambridge: Cambridge University Press.

Billig, M. (1991). *Ideology and opinions*. London: Sage.

Blau, P. (1987). Contrasting theoretical perspectives. In J. Alexander, B. Giesen, R. Munch, & N. Smelser (Eds.), *The micro–macro link* (pp. 71–85). Berkeley: University of California Press.

Boden, D. (1994). *The business of talk*. Cambridge: Polity Press.

Boden, D., & Zimmerman, D. (1991). *Talk and social structure*. Cambridge: Polity Press.

Brecht, B. (1964). The radio as an apparatus of communication. In J. Willett (Ed. and Trans.), *Brecht on theatre: The development of an aesthetic* (pp. 51–53). London: Methuen. (Original work published 1932)

Brenneis, D. (1988). Language and disputing. *Annual Review of Anthropology, 17*, 221–237.

Byrne, P. S., & Long, B. E. L. (1976). *Doctors talking to patients: A study of the verbal behaviours of doctors in the consultation*. London: HMSO.

Carbaugh, D. (1988). *Talking American: Cultural discourses on Donahue*. Norwood, NJ: Ablex.

Cicourel, A. (1981). Notes on the integration of micro- and macro-levels of analysis. In K. Knorr-Cetina & A. V. Cicourel (Eds.), *Advances in social theory and methodology* (pp. 51–80). London: Routledge.

Clark, H., & Haviland, S. (1977). Comprehension and the given-new contract. In R. O. Freedle (Ed.), *Discourse production and comprehension* (pp. 1–40). Hillsdale, NJ: Lawrence Erlbaum Associates.

Clark, H., & Schaefer, E. (1989). Contributing to discourse. *Cognitive Science, 13,* 259–294.

Clayman, S. E. (1988). Displaying neutrality in television news interviews. *Social Problems, 35,* 474–492.

Clayman, S. E. (1992). Footing in the achievement of neutrality: The case of news interview discourse. In P. Drew & J. Heritage (Eds.), *Talk at work: Interaction in institutional settings* (pp. 163–198). Cambridge: Cambridge University Press.

Corsaro, W., & Rizzo, T. (1990). Disputes in the peer culture of American and Italian nursery children. In A. D. Grimshaw (Ed.), *Conflict talk* (pp. 21–66). Cambridge: Cambridge University Press.

Coulter, J. (1982). Remarks on the conceptualization of social structure. *Philosophy of the Social Sciences, 12,* 33–46.

Coulter, J. (1990). Elementary properties of argument sequences. In G. Psathas (Ed.), *Interaction competence* (pp. 181–204). Washington, DC: University Press of America.

Crittenden, J. (1971). Democratic functions of the open mike forum. *Public Opinion Quarterly, 35,* 200–210.

Davidson, J. (1984). Subsequent versions of invitations, offers, requests, and proposals dealing with potential or actual rejection. In J. M. Atkinson & J. Heritage (Eds.), *Structures of social action: Studies in conversation analysis* (pp. 102–128). Cambridge: Cambridge University Press.

Davis, K. (1988). *Power under the microscope.* Dordrecht: Foris.

Drew, P. (1990). Strategies in the contest between witness and lawyer in courtroom cross-examination. In J. Levi & A. G. Walker (Eds.), *Language in the judicial process* (pp. 39–64). New York: Plenum.

Drew, P. (1992). Contested evidence in courtroom cross-examination: The case of a trial for rape. In P. Drew & J. Heritage (Eds.), *Talk at work: Interaction in institutional settings* (pp. 470–520). Cambridge: Cambridge University Press.

Drew, P., & Heritage, J. (1992). Analyzing talk at work: An introduction. In P. Drew & J. Heritage (Eds.), *Talk at work: Interaction in institutional settings* (pp. 3–65). Cambridge: Cambridge University Press.

Drew, P., & Holt, E. (1988). Complainable matters: The use of idiomatic expressions in making complaints. *Social Problems, 35,* 398–417.

Eemeren, F. van, Grootendorst, R., & Kruiger, T. (1987). *Handbook of argumentation theory.* Dordrecht: Foris.

Eisenberg, A., & Garvey, C. (1981). Children's use of verbal strategies in resolving conflicts. *Discourse Processes, 4,* 149–170.

Emlyn-Jones, C. (1987). Speech, the mighty ruler: Persuasion and power in democratic Athens. In J. Hawthorn (Ed.), *Propaganda, persuasion and polemic* (pp. 55–70). London: Edward Arnold.

Fairclough, N. (1989). *Language and power.* London: Longman.

Fisher, S., & Groce, S. (1990). Accounting practices in medical interviews. *Language in Society, 19,* 225–250.

Fisher, S., & Todd, A. D. (Eds.). (1987). *The social organization of doctor–patient communication.* Washington, DC: Center for Applied Linguistics.

Foucault, M. (1977). *Power/knowledge.* Hemel Hempstead: Harvester.

Frankel, R. (1984). From sentence to sequence: Understanding the medical encounter through microinteractional analysis. *Discourse Processes, 7,* 135–170.

Frankel, R. (1990). Talking in interviews: A dispreference for patient-initiated questions in physician–patient encounters. In G. Psathas (Ed.), *Interaction competence* (pp. 231–262). Washington, DC: University Press of America.

Garcia, A. (1991). Dispute resolution without disputing: How the interactional organization of mediation hearings minimizes argument. *American Sociological Review, 56,* 818–835.

Garfinkel, H. (1967). *Studies in ethnomethodology.* Englewood Cliffs, NJ: Prentice-Hall.

Garfinkel, H., & Sacks, H. (1970). On formal structures of practical actions. In J. C. McKinney & E. A. Tiryakian (Eds.), *Theoretical sociology* (pp. 338–366). New York: Appleton-Century-Crofts.

Giddens, A. (1976). *New rules of sociological method.* New York: Basic Books.

Giddens, A. (1979). *Central problems in social theory: Action, structure and contradiction in social analysis.* Berkeley: University of California Press.

Giddens, A. (1981). Agency, institution and time-space analysis. In K. Knorr-Cetina & A. V. Cicourel (Eds.), *Advances in social theory and methodology* (pp. 161–174). London: Routledge.

Giddens, A. (1984). *The constitution of society: Outline of the theory of structuration.* Cambridge: Polity Press.

Gilbert, N., & Mulkay, M. (1984). *Opening Pandora's box: A sociological analysis of scientists' discourse.* Cambridge: Cambridge University Press.

Goffman, E. (1961). *Encounters.* New York: Bobbs-Merrill.

Goffman, E. (1971). *Relations in public.* New York: Basic Books.

Goffman, E. (1981). *Forms of talk.* Oxford: Basil Blackwell.

Goldberg, J. A. (1990). Interrupting the discourse on interruptions: An analysis in terms of relationally neutral, power- and rapport-oriented acts. *Journal of Pragmatics, 14,* 883–903.

Goodwin, C. (1981). *Conversational organization: Interaction between speakers and hearers.* New York: Academic Press.

Goodwin, C. (1986). Between and within: Alternative sequential treatments of continuers and assessments. *Human Studies, 9,* 205–217.

Goodwin, C., & Goodwin, M. H. (1992). Assessments and the construction of context. In A. Duranti & C. Goodwin (Eds.), *Rethinking context* (pp. 151–189). Cambridge: Cambridge University Press.

Goodwin, C., & Heritage, J. (1990). Conversation analysis. *Annual Review of Anthropology, 19,* 283–307.

Goodwin, M. H. (1983). Aggravated correction and disagreement in children's disputes. *Journal of Pragmatics, 7,* 657–677.

Goodwin, M. H. (1990). *He-said-she-said: Talk as social organization among Black children.* Bloomington: Indiana University Press.

Greatbatch, D. (1988). A turn-taking system for British news interviews. *Language in Society, 17,* 401–430.

Greatbatch, D. (1992). On the management of disagreement between news interviewees. In P. Drew & J. Heritage (Eds.), *Talk at work: Interaction in institutional settings* (pp. 268–301). Cambridge: Cambridge University Press.

Grimshaw, A. D. (1990). *Conflict talk.* Cambridge: Cambridge University Press.

Halliday, M. (1978). *Language as social semiotic.* London: Edward Arnold.

Heath, C. (1992). The delivery and reception of diagnosis in the general practice consultation. In P. Drew & J. Heritage (Eds.), *Talk at work: Interaction in institutional settings* (pp. 235–267). Cambridge: Cambridge University Press.

Heritage, J. (1984). *Garfinkel and ethnomethodology.* Cambridge: Polity Press.

Heritage, J. (1985). Analyzing news interviews: Aspects of the production of talk for an overhearing audience. In T. van Dijk (Ed.), *Handbook of discourse analysis* (Vol. 3, pp. 95–119). London: Academic Press.

Heritage, J. (1989). Current developments in conversation analysis. In D. Roger & P. Bull (Eds.), *Conversation* (pp. 21–47). Clevedon: Multilingual Matters.

Heritage, J., & Greatbatch, D. (1986). Generating applause: A study of rhetoric and response at party political conferences. *American Journal of Sociology, 19,* 110–157.

Heritage, J., & Greatbatch, D. (1991). On the institutional character of institutional talk: The case of news interviews. In D. Boden & D. Zimmerman (Eds.), *Talk and social structure* (pp. 93–137). Cambridge: Polity Press.

Heritage, J., & Sefi, S. (1992). Dilemmas of advice: Aspects of the delivery and reception of advice in interactions between health visitors and first time mothers. In P. Drew & J. Heritage (Eds.), *Talk at work: Interaction in institutional settings* (pp. 359–417). Cambridge: Cambridge University Press.

Heritage, J., & Watson, D. R. (1979). Formulations as conversational objects. In G. Psathas (Ed.), *Everyday language: Studies in ethnomethodology* (pp. 123–162). Hillsdale, NJ: Lawrence Erlbaum Associates.

Houtkoop-Steenstra, H. (1991). Opening sequences in Dutch telephone conversation. In D. Boden & D. Zimmerman (Eds.), *Talk and social structure* (pp. 232–250). Cambridge: Polity Press.

Hutchby, I. (1995). Aspects of recipient design in expert advice-giving on call in radio. *Discourse Processes, 19,* 219–238.

Hutchby, I., & Drew, P. (1995). Conversation analysis. In J.-O. Ostman, J. Verschueren, & J. Blommaert (Eds.), *Handbook of pragmatics* (pp. 282–289). Amsterdam: John Benjamins.

Hutchby, I., & Wooffitt, R. (in press). *Conversation analysis: An introduction.* Cambridge: Polity Press.

Jacobs, S., & Jackson, S. (1981). Argument as a natural category: The routine grounds for arguing in conversation. *Western Journal of Speech Communication, 45,* 118–132.

Jefferson, G. (1978). Sequential aspects of storytelling in conversation. In J. Schenkein (Ed.), *Studies in the organization of conversational interaction* (pp. 219–248). New York: Academic Press.

Jefferson, G. (1981). *The abominable "ne?": A working paper exploring the phenomenon of post-response pursuit of response* (Occasional Paper No. 6). Manchester, UK: University of Manchester, Department of Sociology.

Jefferson, G. (1986). Notes on latency in overlap onset. *Human Studies, 9,* 153–183.

Jefferson, G., & Schegloff, E. A. (1975). *Sketch: Some orderly aspects of overlap in natural conversation.* Paper presented at the Meetings of the American Anthropological Association.

Kopperschmidt, J. (1985). An analysis of argumentation. In T. van Dijk (Ed.), *Handbook of discourse analysis* (Vol. 2, pp. 159–168). London: Academic Press.

Kotthoff, H. (1993). Disagreement and concession in disputes: On the context-sensitivity of preference structures. *Language in Society, 22,* 193–216.

Labov, W. (1972). The transformation of experience in narrative syntax. In W. Labov, *Language in the inner city: Studies in the Black English vernacular* (pp. 354–396). Philadelphia: Philadelphia University Press.

Labov, W., & Waletsky, J. (1967). Narrative analysis: Oral versions of personal experience. In J. Helm (Ed.), *Essays on the verbal and visual arts* (pp. 12–44). Seattle: University of Washington Press.

Lee, J. R. E. (1987). Prologue: Talking organization. In G. Button & J. R. E. Lee (Eds), *Talk and social organization* (pp. 19–53). Clevedon: Multilingual Matters.

Lein, L., & Brenneis, D. (1978). Children's disputes in three speech communities. *Language in Society, 7,* 299–323.

Levinson, S. (1983). *Pragmatics.* Cambridge: Cambridge University Press.

Linell, P., & Luckmann, T. (1991). Asymmetries in dialogue: Some conceptual preliminaries. In I. Markova & K. Foppa (Eds.), *Asymmetries in dialogue* (pp. 1–20). Hemel Hempstead: Harvester Wheatsheaf.

Livingstone, S., & Lunt, P. (1994). *Talk on television.* London: Routledge.

Maynard, D. W. (1985). How children start arguments. *Language in Society, 14,* 1–30.

Maynard, D. W. (1986). The development of argumentative skills among children. In A. Adler & P. Adler (Eds.), *Sociological studies of child development* (Vol. 1, pp. 233–258). Greenwich, CT: JAI Press.

Maynard, D. W. (1991). Interaction and asymmetry in clinical discourse. *American Journal of Sociology, 97,* 448–495.

McHoul, A. (1978). The organization of turns at formal talk in the classroom. *Language in Society, 19,* 183–213.

Moerman, M. (1988). *Talking culture: Ethnography and conversation analysis.* Philadelphia: University of Pennsylvania Press.

Moss, P., & Higgins, C. (1984). Radio voices. *Media, Culture and Society, 6,* 353–375.

Mulkay, M. (1986). Agreement and disagreement in conversations and letters. *Text, 5,* 201–227.

Ochs, E. (1988). *Culture and language development.* Cambridge: Cambridge University Press.

O'Keefe, D. J. (1977). Two concepts of argument. *Journal of the American Forensic Association, 13,* 121–128.

Perakyla, A., & Silverman, D. (1991). Reinterpreting speech exchange systems: Communication formats in AIDS counselling. *Sociology, 25,* 627–651.

Perelman, C., & Olbrechts-Tyteca, L. (1971). *The new rhetoric.* Notre Dame, IN: University of Notre Dame Press.

Pollner, M. (1987). *Mundane reason.* Cambridge: Cambridge University Press.

Pomerantz, A. (1978). Compliment responses: Notes on the cooperation of multiple constraints. In J. Schenkein (Ed.), *Studies in the organization of conversational interaction* (pp. 79–112). New York: Academic Press.

Pomerantz, A. (1984a). Agreeing and disagreeing with assessments: Some features of preferred/dispreferred turn-shapes. In J. M. Atkinson & J. Heritage (Eds.), *Structures of social action: Studies in conversation analysis* (pp. 57–101). Cambridge: Cambridge University Press.

Pomerantz, A. (1984b). Giving a source or basis: The practice in conversation of telling "how I know." *Journal of Pragmatics, 8,* 607–625.

Pomerantz, A. (1986). Extreme case formulations. *Human Studies, 9,* 219–230.

Pomerantz, A. (1988–1989). Constructing skepticism: Four devices for engendering the audience's skepticism. *Research on Language and Social Interaction, 22,* 293–313.

Purves, L. (1991, January 4–10). The rudest man on radio? *Radio Times,* pp. 18–19.

Rancer, A., Miles, T., & Baukus, R. (1994, April). *Communicative predispositions and demographic characteristics of listeners and non-listeners to talk radio.* Paper presented at the Annual Meeting of the Eastern Communication Association, Washington, DC.

Sacks, H. (1963). Sociological description. *Berkeley Journal of Sociology, 8,* 1–16.

Sacks, H. (1984). Notes on methodology. In J. M. Atkinson & J. Heritage (Eds.), *Structures of social action: Studies in conversation analysis* (pp. 21–27). Cambridge: Cambridge University Press.

Sacks, H. (1987). On the preferences for agreement and contiguity in sequences in conversation. In G. Button & J. R. E. Lee (Eds.), *Talk and social organization* (pp. 54–69). Clevedon: Multilingual Matters.

Sacks, H. (1992). *Lectures on conversation* (Vols. 1 & 2). Oxford: Basil Blackwell.

Sacks, H., Schegloff, E. A., & Jefferson, G. (1974). A simplest systematics for the organization of turn-taking for conversation. *Language, 50,* 696–735.

Scannell, P. (1991). Introduction: The relevance of talk. In P. Scannell (Ed.), *Broadcast talk* (pp. 1–13). London: Sage.

Schegloff, E. A. (1968). Sequencing in conversational openings. *American Anthropologist, 70,* 1075–1095.

Schegloff, E. A. (1982). Discourse as an interactional achievement: Some uses of "uh huh" and other things that come between sentences. In D. Tannen (Ed.), *Analyzing discourse: Text and talk* (pp. 71–93). Washington, DC: Georgetown University Press.

Schegloff, E. A. (1987). Recycled turn-beginnings. In G. Button & J. R. E. Lee (Eds.), *Talk and social organization* (pp. 70–85). Clevedon: Multilingual Matters.

Schegloff, E. A. (1988–1989). From interview to confrontation: Observations on the Bush/Rather encounter. *Research on Language and Social Interaction, 22,* 215–240.

Schegloff, E. A. (1991). Reflections on talk and social structure. In D. Boden & D. Zimmerman (Eds.), *Talk and social structure* (pp. 44–70). Cambridge: Polity Press.

Schegloff, E. A. (1992). Repair after next turn: The last structurally provided defense of intersubjectivity in conversation. *American Journal of Sociology, 97,* 1295–1345.

Schegloff, E. A., Jefferson, G., & Sacks, H. (1977). The preference for self-correction in the organization of repair in conversation. *Language, 53,* 361–382.

Schegloff, E. A., & Sacks, H. (1973). Opening up closings. *Semiotica, 7,* 289–327.

Schiffrin, D. (1985). Everyday argument: The organization of diversity in talk. In T. A. van Dijk (Ed.), *Handbook of discourse analysis* (Vol. 3, pp. 35–46). London: Academic Press.

Silverman, D. (1987). *Communication and medical practice: Social relations in the clinic.* London: Sage.

Smith, D. (1978). "K" is mentally ill: The anatomy of a factual account. *Sociology, 12,* 23–53.

Step, M., & Rubin, A. (1994, April). *Is the viewer there? Audience activity and daytime television talk shows.* Paper presented at the Annual Meetings of the Eastern Communication Association, Washington, DC.

Talbot, M. (1992). "I wish you'd stop interrupting me!": Interruptions and asymmetries in speaker rights in equal encounters. *Journal of Pragmatics, 16,* 451–466.

Thompson, J. B. (1984). *Studies in the theory of ideology.* Cambridge: Polity Press.

Thornborrow, J. (1991). Orderly discourse and background knowledge. *Text, 11,* 581–606.

Toulmin, S. (1958). *The uses of argument.* Cambridge: Cambridge University Press.

Turow, J. (1974). Talk radio as interpersonal communication. *Journal of Broadcasting, 18,* 171–179.

Verwey, N. E. (1990). *Radio call-ins and covert politics.* Avebury: Gower.

Vuchinich, S. (1990). The sequential organization of closing in verbal family conflict. In A. D. Grimshaw (Ed.), *Conflict talk* (pp. 118–138). Cambridge: Cambridge University Press.

Watson, D. R. (1990). Some features of the elicitation of confessions in murder interrogations. In G. Psathas (Ed.), *Interaction competence* (pp. 263–295). Washington, DC: University Press of America.

West, C., & Zimmerman, D. (1977). Women's place in everyday talk: Reflections on parent–child interaction. *Social Problems, 24,* 521–529.

West, C., & Zimmerman, D. (1983). Small insults: The study of interruptions in cross-sex conversations between unacquainted persons. In B. Thorne, C. Kramerae, & N. Henley (Eds.), *Language, gender and society* (pp. 102–117). Rowley: Newbury House.

Whalen, M., & Zimmerman, D. (1987). Sequential and institutional contexts in calls for help. *Social Psychology Quarterly, 50,* 172–185.

Witten, M. (1992). The restriction of meaning in religious discourse: Centripetal devices in a fundamentalist Christian sermon. In R. Wuthnow (Ed.), *Vocabularies of public life* (pp. 19–38). London: Routledge.

Zimmerman, D., & Boden, D. (1991). Structure-in-action: An introduction. In D. Boden & D. Zimmerman (Eds.), *Talk and social structure* (pp. 3–21). Cambridge: Polity Press.

Zimmerman, D., & Pollner, M. (1971). The everyday word as a phenomenon. In J. D. Douglas (Ed.), *Understanding everyday life* (pp. 80–103). London: Routledge.

Author and Subject Index